Parnell and Irish Nationalism

Parnell
and Irish
Nationalism

Michael Hurst

Fellow in Modern History and Politics, St. John's
College, Oxford

Routledge & Kegan Paul London

First published 1968
by Routledge & Kegan Paul Ltd
Broadway House, 68–74 Carter Lane
London, E.C.4

Printed in Great Britain
by Western Printing Services Ltd
Bristol

© *Michael Hurst 1968*

SBN 7100 2901 2

To James Campbell

Contents

'No man has a right to fix the boundary of the march of a nation; no man has a right to say to his country—thus far shalt thou go and no further.'

Charles Stewart Parnell at Cork,
21 January 1885

Introduction

A cool appraisal of Parnell as an Irish nationalist is something calculated to raise as much self-righteous hubbub in the Republic of Ireland as would one of Sir Winston Churchill as a statesman in the United Kingdom. The fact that one man died in 1891 and the other in 1964 is the measure of the different scales of judgment circumstances have decreed for the two countries. Across the Irish Sea men who actually pride themselves upon a capacity for empirical approaches to historical subjects bridle at any original observations on such an important political saint as the great Parnell, huff and puff about 'unjustified conclusions', and resentfully deplore that such 'abominable distortions' should see the light of the printing works. As in many unhappy bigot-ridden nations, there is in Ireland a widespread feeling that only Irishmen (including for some reason the resented Ulstermen) are entitled to talk and write about Irish history. The foreigner just does not understand. Perhaps the truth of the matter is that he understands too well and while in the process of explaining exposes many a prejudice cherished by one at least of the factions to be found on both sides of the border. These remarks do not apply only to extremists. Moderates lamenting the supercession of the old Irish Nationalist Party are as prickly about Parnell as devotees of the Irish Republican Army, and Unionists of most shades preserve for him a dislike as profound as the liking among their opponents.

Ironically, the Irish past often generates more heat among Irishmen than the Irish present. When tariff barriers are being lowered between the Republic and the United Kingdom, when an Ulster extremist, albeit a Presbyterian clergyman like Ian Paisley, is cast into prison for being 'plus royaliste que le roi', when Eddie McAteer feels able at Rostrevor to declare that Northern Ireland should go on existing while the bulk of Ulster Protestants feel it should, it would appear that the once all-powerful bigotry of Ireland is at last on the wane. European oecumenicalism has apparently stabbed both Catholic and Protestant zealots in the back throughout the island and although resistance against change is often extremely strong, the impetus behind amelioration is very formidable. Economic common-sense has at last prevailed in many a Nationalist and Unionist mind and autarchy well and truly displaced as a long-term ideal. New generations have accepted the Belfast or Dublin versions of the past, but seen no cause for basing their current behaviour upon them. All this must not be seen as a completed process of enlightenment however. Some things can take an unconscionable time a-waning. But many Irish historians have sought to escape from the shade of priest and presbyter and produced work of a truly detached kind. Maybe the 'enlightenment' will spread from the professionals down through the population to the less distinguished gentlemen and players. One important fault, nevertheless, has run through much of this writing—excessive caution, engendering a species of intellectual anaemia. The British are no longer all that was bad, or all that was glorious, the Catholic masses and Ulster Protestants are neither denigrated nor lauded with the same abandon as in the past, and the 'Ascendancy' is analysed rather than abused. Yet everything was not of a colour between dark grey and off-white. There were villains and heroes. Nor should the force of circumstantial evidence and telling intellectual analysis be neglected in a sea of documented fact. Some of the scholars concerned tend not to see the bog for the weeds.

The history, first of England and Ireland, and then of Britain and Ireland, makes very depressing reading. Yet it is more than a mere example of the big conquering the small. More than bare greed led England to tamper with her western neighbour. The security question always loomed large in the minds of the London statesmen well before the Reformation complicated what had previously been a comparatively simple clash of political sentiments and interests. Only the development of the latest weapons has finally rendered it obsolete. Once the supporters of James II signed the Treaty of Limerick on 3rd. October, 1691 the old almost chaotic arrangements surrounding London's control of Ireland passed away. Cromwell had foreshadowed what followed, but had failed to perpetuate his policies. Now, when the toleration clauses of Limerick were cast to the winds by ruthless victors, there began the period of the penal laws which, for the first time in a

truly sustained fashion, created an almost absolute identifica-
tion between Irish national aspirations and the Catholic
Church on the one hand and between support for the British
connection and Protestantism on the other. Retention of a
separate Irish Parliament in the leading strings of London
and composed of Protestants meant, however, that a symbol
of national separations lived on. As with many nationalities on
the continent, the destruction of the 'nationalistic' sections of
the ruling and middle class left the peasantry as the leading
repositories of national feeling, a feeling automatically
associated with their especial interests. Foremost amongst
these, of course, was the land and the problems surrounding its
ownership and use. English land law was applied by the new
régime with particular thoroughness and gave the ordinary
peasant far less independence than the native Brehon law,
with its recognition of tribal or clan common rights. Hence
the passion for land for oneself, free from landlord control,
remained a cardinal aspect of Irish national self-assertion and
down to Parnell's day provided the prime motive force behind
mass protest against London rule. An already powerful
religion acquired an even added authority as it offered aid and
comfort amidst its own adversity. Moreover, London's
enemies were more often than not Catholic and sympathetic
to Ireland's cause. To them thousands of Irishmen flocked for
service on the field of battle. One such refugee was an ancestor
of President de Gaulle. Through emigration the old Catholic
upper class of both native Irish and old English origin kept
partly together, but war and the ravages of time eventually
prevented the survival of a cadre ready to return home and
lead rebellion. In any case, except in most unusual circum-

stances, Ireland's geographical position was such that any rebellion was certain to be crushed by British and Anglo-Irish settler might. London feared for her security, yet was generally able to secure it. Ownership of Ireland simply minimized risks.

As the eighteenth century progressed the intensity of the penal system against Catholics gradually lessened. At the same time chronic discontent amongst the Irish-based aristocracy, gentry and merchant classes and the mass colonial settlements of Ulster developed against the exploitation of Ireland's economy as the price for political support. And the situation was given an added poignancy by the full political and economic Union between England and Scotland contracted in 1707. When grievances of a similar kind brought on rebellion in the thirteen North American colonies, Protestant Ireland was largely united in bidding for more political and economic independence. So in 1782 from the aristocracy down to Ulster farm labourers, from Anglicans and Presbyterians to Quakers, Protestant Ireland secured a 'New Deal' and there began the period of what is commonly known as 'Grattan's Parliament'. Britain, embarrassed, had meant Ireland strong. The British argument about security was clinched by a practical proof. Nevertheless, the Grattanites' politics were a far cry from those of the emigrants, or 'Wild Geese', and consisted of something about half-way between the Washingtonian and Mackenzie King schools of colonial nationalism. Nor were the British reduced to anything approaching impotence in Irish affairs. Quite the contrary, for although the Dublin Parliament now prepared its own menu, the Crown gave its consent to legislation on the advice of its

British ministers. Tariffs also remained to hinder the entry of Irish goods into Britain.

Along with Protestant self-assertion against London went a further liberalization of the penal laws; a process much accelerated by the impact of the French Revolution upon Protestant-Catholic relations in the British Isles generally. Some Protestants, notably Whigs like Grattan himself, favoured the granting of full Catholic Emancipation—that is, going on from franchise and ecclesiastical concessions to allowing a virtually unrestricted holding of official positions and membership of Parliament by Catholics. Numerous optimists hoped that when official monetary aid for the new Maynooth College or seminary, built to educate and train men previously sent to the continent was forthcoming, a period of general reconciliation might set in. By sheer force of circumstances numerous parish priests had become popular leaders and under the new arrangements it was hoped their influence would be used to bring about a gradual acceptance of the political status quo and Irish national solidarity. That this failed to materialize is hardly surprising when the longstanding nature of the disputes and great intensity of feeling surrounding them are borne in mind. Although many among the peasantry became forty-shilling freeholder voters they remained so much polling fodder at elections and nothing happened to moderate the extraordinary abuses that had grown up in the Irish land system. Tenants' improvements went uncompensated, the land hunger and landlord absenteeism went on unabated and the notorious middlemen throve on their ill-gotten gains. The passion for a piece of land continued to flourish among the Catholic masses and essentially local terrorism called Ribbonism, run on lines reminiscent of the Mafia, frequently disturbed most counties outside the areas of the north-east, where Protestant settlement was widespread. In fact the liberal Protestants offered the Catholic masses little they really cared for. The Grattanite pedigrees were those of the oppressor, the landlord remained paramount and the English land law was the only system with authority—and in a debased form at that. Initially, nothing existed in Ireland capable of linking together all the discordant elements among the Catholics, but with the foundation of the United Irishmen things changed fast. The initiative behind this organization came at first from frustrated Protestants, particularly those in Ulster despairing of reform from the new constitution. After a few years of constitutionalism from 1791 until 1794 it became a secret military organization aiming at revolution. Its inspiration was at once American and French and gradually its tentacles spread over the country among the discontented of both Catholic and Protestant persuasions. Like many moderates before and since, Henry Grattan was to discover that liberalism in slow motion rapidly loses the initiative in essentially illiberal societies where various kinds of extremism can muster mass support outside constitutional limits. While the outcome of the plotting—the rebellion of 1798—was in the actual event something of a damp squib, the fact of its occurrence at all and the element of French participation persuaded the British government that the Grattan experiment could hardly continue and that only a drastic change would secure any chance of lasting success.

The panacea favoured by the Younger Pitt and actually applied was a legislative Union between Britain and Ireland.

As originally envisaged the operation was to be one of give and take. As it turned out the give in most respects was Irish and the take British. Charges that the British government provoked the 1798 affair to open up the way for a Union are almost certainly baseless. That it took decisive action to minimize the outbreak is more to the point. But perhaps the most significant aspect of the whole sorry story was the defection of the northern Republicans from the revolutionary cause in the face of growing Catholic power among the United Irishmen. Nor was the very slight involvement of the lower clergy in as much as sedition, let alone full-scale rebellion, an encouraging factor for the rebels. With the overwhelming proportion of Protestants now loyal and the Catholic hierarchy open to a deal, Pitt deputed Castlereagh to persuade the Irish Parliament to commit suicide and acquire the agreement of the Catholics to a Union by indicating that it would be accompanied by Emancipation proper. At first sight too the financial proposals looked quite tempting. With great difficulty the Union law was got through the Dublin House of Commons and the two countries became officially one after the Lords and the Crown had given their approval. But, and it was a very big but, the moral obligation to grant Catholic Emancipation was ignored. Not only did the new statute proclaim the permanent establishment of the Anglican Church of Ireland, but nothing else was changed to please the Catholic three-quarters of the population as such. 1800 no more than 1782 was to prove a starting point for reconciliation between Britain and Ireland, or between the factions within Ireland.

Whether Emancipation at the point of Union would have done the trick is very much open to doubt. Possibly a great many of the new Catholic middle class, which had sprung into being in the Grattan period, might have rallied to the loyal cause; likewise the small Catholic section of the aristocracy and gentry and many among the higher Catholic clergy. But the vast majority of the Catholic peasantry would almost certainly have remained at best inactively hostile, aided and abetted by certain of the Maynooth educated young clergy, whose humble origins gave them a nationalistic bent and whose training and environment had involved the imbibing of British ideals of freedom applied to the Irish scene. Orangemen among the northern Protestants would have been outraged at the concession and the revived loyalty among erstwhile Protestant Republicans might well have wilted somewhat. Still whether or not this had happened, inter-Irish denominational and faction relationships would have remained in a sorry state.

As things were, the Union began with a first-class Catholic grievance to threaten it. Round this grievance all Catholic resentment against the British, the landlords, and Protestantism generally could gather. Minor concessions made no appreciable change in the situation and for a time the Irish parliamentary body remained largely unrepresentative of the mass of county electors outside of Ulster and a limited number of other small areas. Well before Daniel O'Connell contrived to set his Catholic Association going in 1824 and provided a constitutional replacement for the unconstitutional United Irishmen as a link between all sections of chronically discontented Catholics and the more extreme radicals among the Protestants, all manner of trouble had attended the new régime. The gradual introduction of free trade and the burden of Ireland's agreed portion of the National Debt bore hard upon an economy which had burgeoned considerably under the 1782 arrangement. Abuses on the land from the owners' side continued in full force, while the passion for subdivision on that of the peasantry aggravated an often desperate situation. Actual famine nurtured fresh resentment and the priesthood more often than not provided the leadership which directed the grievances to a central point, instead of allowing them to be worked out as part of local vendettas. Public disorder was chronic, yet many liberally inclined Protestants wanted or worked for Catholic Emancipation, or even went so far as to share the widespread Catholic desire to see the Union repealed. A large proportion of the British Tories, in and out of the Cabinet, were liberal in inclination. Almost the whole of Whiggery felt the same way. The major obstacles were British and Irish ultra-Protestant opinion and the refusal by the Catholics to accept a compromise settlement whereby Irish Catholicism became something akin to a second established Church backed by government money. The latter illustrates very well the basic insolubility of the most fundamental difficulty—the profound feeling of national separateness linked to a yearning for Irish independence and its inevitable clash with British and settler pretensions. Tempted though it was to consent to the British suggestion, the Catholic hierarchy feared such a course would lose the Church and its priesthood the firm hold enjoyed over the majority of Irishmen. And if conciliation could not really begin at the top for fear of the bottom, and if the bottom could not be contacted adequately except through the top, the outlook for London and the moderates was bleak indeed.

Once O'Connell's movement tried to become more than an urban middle class affair and to embrace all classes, it caught on at once. The priests linked up with the Catholic middle classes, business and professional, living in the larger towns and supplied the overall organizational network of nationalistic contacts these groups could never have mustered on their own. Cash as well as enthusiasm flowed in from the poorest sections of the peasantry, for though O'Connell and many of his closest associates were landlords and envisaged an Ireland relatively static on the social and economic sides, a common national and religious sentiment bound the people to them. Nevertheless, it was the liberal Protestants who were the first to exploit the ground he had prepared, for while Emancipation remained ungranted only Protestants could legally stand for Parliament. In the general election of 1826 many peasant voters of several important counties declined to serve again as lobby fodder and voted for outside Protestant figures, almost invariably landlords who favoured immediate Emancipation. Emboldened by their success, O'Connell himself contested a by-election in County Clare and drubbed an opponent, who though a ministerialist, favoured the Emancipation cause. That was in 1828 and the next year Emancipation was achieved, or at least, went onto the statute book. But the victory was a heavily qualified one. The Catholic Association was declared illegal and the minimum franchise qualification raised to ten pounds. In other words the technical ground upon which the Irish majority was now being discriminated against was ostensibly economic, not religious, and the hierarchy and higher clergy, and the Catholic aristocracy and gentry, a portion of the Catholic middle class and a great many of the liberal Protestants were now likely to discountenance further radical political and social change.

The demand for the granting of Catholic Emancipation had not been a bid for full religious equality. Removal of Catholic disabilities was a very different proposition from removal of Church of Ireland privileges like establishment and tithes, yet for real equality such privileges would have to go. But O'Connell's next moves were even more fundamental in their aims. Tithe was attacked as an important instance of 'Ascendancy' injustice. Nevertheless, it was completely put in the shade by the Repeal campaign, which called for a restoration of the Grattanite constitution. With varying degrees of intensity this phase of O'Connell's career lasted from 1830 until his death in 1847. Probably the most important aspect of the whole affair was the presence of an 'Irish' Repeal party at Westminster. Following upon Emancipation the 1830 general election saw the return to Parliament of a group of members favouring Repeal and other measures designed to remove Catholic discontents, or satisfy middle class radical aspirations. As with Emancipation, so with Repeal; the gulf between the leadership and the masses was glossed over by a common feeling against London and its Dublin Castle agents. A great irony surrounding Repeal politics was that without British law and order they would not have been possible. 1798 had shown that Grattanism on its own was bankrupt, and Emancipation in itself would not have altered the agrarian question and the emotional national and social problems surrounding it. As it was, a physical force side of nationalism did assert itself to some extent in the 'Young Ireland' movement—a rebellious breakaway organization sick to death of

O'Connell's unwavering constitutionalism—and demonstrated its existence in the melancholy outbreak of 1848. Generally speaking, however, O'Connell did maintain a strong grip upon 'Patriots' to the end of his days.

The vital result of having an 'Irish' parliamentary party was that when it came to hold the balance in the House of Commons, O'Connell was able to exact a price on secondary and tertiary issues from the Whigs and their British allies. Here was a precedent Parnell was later to take much further and apply in his bid for Home Rule, but at the point—1835—when it first came about British opinion was well nigh unanimous against Repeal and there was no pushing beyond poor law, tithe and municipal corporation reform. During the second half of the decade of Whig government, begun in the last months of 1830, Emancipation was made a reality in Irish public appointments. Peel abandoned this process and the ineffectual character of a much-reduced Repeal party at Westminster made reversion to a more colonial style administration all the easier. Conservative victory in 1841 did a lot to stymie what Emancipation and the 1832 Reform Act had done to aid the 'Irish' cause. Meanwhile, among the nationalistic Irish, temptations to indulge in violence increased sharply, and among some of the more liberal-minded Protestants with Radical opinions on land questions a Federalist concept grew up, which some thought would enable 'Orange' and 'Green' Irishmen to become mutually reconciled with each other and with Britain. At the very time when O'Connell was under attack from the nationalistic left, anxious to throw off both his moderation and Catholic alignment, he was fascinated by the prospect of a Federalist way of persuading the British to be 'reasonable'. That he hesitated, albeit temporarily, between Federalism and Repeal was more a strong indication of his sense of proportion than one of fickleness, as his enemies on the left suggested. Almost at once under the pressure from his party, he reverted to full Repeal, and Federalism was relegated to the background for about a quarter of a century.

By 1840 the first flush of Repealer strength was fading away. Weakness of social and economic links between the party leadership and the masses, the narrowness of the franchise and the lure of British ways and rewards, plus the alarm felt by some sections of the Irish Catholic middle class at the prospect of a genuine social revolution, all made for a weakening of the electoral appeal of O'Connell and the enthusiasm behind him. The general elections of 1841 and 1847 saw his party relegated to the backward areas of the west, but in 1845 there began the great famine which was to ravage Ireland for more than three years and make party politics seem temporarily something of an irrelevance.

Throughout the Union period the population of Ireland had been rocketing upwards. From just over five millions in 1800 it had reached eight and a quarter millions by 1845. In 1851 it was down to six and a half millions. Death and emigration were jointly responsible for the drop and throughout Ireland, the United States and Australia, not to mention Britain itself, Catholic Irishmen bore a bitter resentment against the London government and the Union generally for something they themselves were partly to blame for. Great though the evils of the Irish land system were, none were more harmful to Ireland than the passion for sub-division, overconcentration upon the potato and the resistance almost invariably offered to improving landlords. Nevertheless, suffering and passion, and the legacy of the past, blinded most Catholics to the truth, even where intelligence and education had made appreciation of it possible. Among the masses generally there was absolutely no hope of anything except renewed hate and exacerbated national feeling, despite the good work done by Anglican clergy and Ascendancy landlords to ease the disaster. The blunders of a *laissez-faire* administration erased any incipient gratitude among the poor.

Initially, the consequence of the catastrophe was a political vacuum. Into it came two constructive influences working against sectarian strife. One was the educational system, which discouraged national animosity against the Protestants and their British backers. The other was a land reform movement, which, while attempting to bridge the gap between the Irish factions, did not set out to stimulate Irish feeling in favour of legislative separation from London. On the contrary, it sought to fit Irish patriotism within a United Kingdom framework. In many ways the men behind the tenant right campaign shared the outlook of the Federalists, or were themselves supporters of the Federal cause. Official legislation after the famine had not touched the problem of the peasant preoccupation with the land and the switchover to grazing by many of the new landlords, who had bought out their bankrupted predecessors under the provisions of the Encumbered Estates Act, had recreated a land shortage for the poorer agricultural classes. Rebellion, discredited by the 1848 fiasco, was clearly out, so the population looked on while an enlightened minority attempted to have the privileges enjoyed by the Ulster cultivators extended to the whole of Ireland.

In 1850 an Irish 'Independent Brigade' based on these ideas sprang into being among some of the members of parliament and prospered in the 1852 general election. It was but a short-lived affair and in no way sustained by the county franchise extension of two years before. Sectarian strife ruined the tenant right organization and place-hunting, coupled with poor leadership and failure to impress the British soon led to the disintegration of the party. The ball was back in the court of the direct-action men. Young Ireland and 1848 enjoyed the warm approval of the Catholic masses—a fact which was eventually exploited.

The motive force for this came in the first instance from the United States, where numerous embittered immigrants were thirsting for British blood. Foremost among the enthusiastic spirits behind the new move were James Stephens and John O'Mahony, two of the younger rebels of 1848, the former of whom returned to Ireland in 1858 and with the encouragement of the latter, at that time in New York, founded the Fenian movement. This was a brotherhood of oath-bound members, pledged to overthrow British authority in Ireland. All recourse to constitutional action was condemned. There was no social programme to provide an added attraction or distraction. Such a thing was to wait upon the achievement of independence, which was to be 'Soon or never'. And, in fact, the blanket nature of the society's aim maximised support—a support Cardinal Cullen's rival National Association did little or nothing to reduce. A year after the Cardinal made his counter-bid for constitutionalism with a programme of land reform, disestablishment of the Church of Ireland and denominational education, Stephens decided that the time had arrived for rebellion. The United States Civil War had just ended and a certain number of experienced Irish officers from both sides had offered him their services. But the British had been well-served by informers and struck rapidly and hard. Numerous arrests were made, *Habeas Corpus* was suspended in 1866 and much of the movement broken up. When an outbreak did occur, in March 1867, it proved an even greater fiasco than 1848. That Fenianism survived at all was due to the immense force of national feeling among the smallest farmers and labourers from the Catholic masses. Curiously enough, though, a short term consequence of the troubles was to accelerate the virtual acceptance of much of the Cullen programme by the Whig-Liberals. An important part in bringing this about was played by the trial, imprisonment and rescue or attempted rescue of Fenian prisoners. These prisoners, known as the 'Manchester Martyrs', had killed a policeman while rescuing two of their comrades and did the Irish cause generally a power of good, albeit in ways they scarcely intended.

The lull in Irish national agitation had been largely unavoidable in view of the fundamental blow delivered to the whole fabric of peasant society by the great famine, yet improvement in the economic condition of the country had also helped to keep things quieter. The British nevertheless soon spotted the change and promptly extended to Ireland taxes hitherto reserved for themselves. An income tax and a higher spirit duty were inevitably unpopular and with the economic decline of the 1860's certainly contributed towards pushing many of the peasants into the arms of the Fenians. Where they were too poor to pay income tax, they always had a grievance about the spirit duty. The Fenians in a weakened condition were hardly in a position to strike again, so on a short-term basis Liberal candidates reaped a handsome harvest once Gladstone took up Irish Church disestablishment, land reform and education as his own causes. However nationalistic a priest, he would not look such magnificent gift horses in the mouth. The Catholic Church generally therefore gave its wholehearted support to Liberal candidates at the 1868 general election, with the result that it was just as much a Liberal triumph in Ireland as in the rest of the United Kingdom. Of course, the electors were not drawn from the poorest Irish Catholic classes, yet, as immediately subsequent history was to show, they were not by any means basically unsympathetic to much of the Fenian message, even though many of them preferred quieter and more practical methods of seeing it realized than the head-on collisions with British might recommended by the movement's zealots. The physical force party again received a fillip from the disappointing way in which the British government implemented its promises to the moderate Irish groups. Too much wealth remained in Church of Ireland hands after disestablishment for Fenian liking; land reform brought merely compensation for improvements and a very modest opening for land purchase by peasants—the three F's of fair rent, fixity of tenure and free sale remaining the privileges of Ulster; and Gladstone's bid to solve the vexed university question foundered on the rock of sectarian strife and temporarily destroyed his government. All three problems, and especially the last, illustrated perfectly the dilemma of any liberally inclined British administration. Domestic opinion in Britain generally prevented using solutions likely to satisfy

18

Irish Catholic opinion and what resulted was almost certain to be at best a compromise. Happily for Gladstone not only the Fenian grouping revived under the strains set up by disappointed hopes, for under Isaac Butt the Federalist cause picked up and made the pace in a new Home Rule party in Parliament.

Between 1869 and 1872, before secret ballot was introduced, various Home Rule candidates were successful in Irish by-elections. Conservatives and Liberals alike fell their victims. In 1870 Butt formed the Home Government Association, a body drawing an amount of support from members of the Protestant minority disillusioned with the British after Irish Church disestablishment and, like the Fenians, concerned to attain a sole object—Home Rule within a federal framework. Nevertheless, as with other 'Orange-Green' bodies the common feeling soon withered, though Butt, a former Conservative, remained to lead the new party both in Ireland and at Westminster when it took on an increasingly 'Green' complexion. Some of the new Home Rulers were simply frightened Liberals, but others had a genuine concern to win through and enjoyed the sympathy of many Fenians, largely because of the efforts made by men like Butt to secure amnesty for Fenian political prisoners. A suspended judgment restrained the physical force party as they watched to see what success Butt would have. By 1873 he felt the time was ripe to go all out for a Home Rule League dominated by groups committed to the side of the Catholic masses on most basic social and economic questions. Another Kaunda-Smith coalition was stone dead.

Franchise extension in Ireland under the 1868 Act had

made but scant impact upon the political scene. In Britain the 1867 Acts had, however, brought new advantages to the Irish, whether 'Orange' or 'Green'. For the first time large numbers of immigrants and their descendants went on to the electoral rolls and Irish influence at Westminster could be exerted both through Irish M.P.'s and the pressure groups of voters could exercise over non-Irish M.P.'s by making themselves hard to get in the constituencies. It so happened that the 'Green' Irish were by far the larger faction, so their influence was accordingly the greater. In fact, of course, it needed to be, for the spontaneous sympathies of most British statesmen, politicians and electors were with the Unionist cause the 'Orange' faction stood for. Even radical reformers made the continuance of Union the real basis of their Irish policies and the task the Greenites had before them was formidable indeed. Had persuasion by argument been their only weapon, progress would have been virtually non-existent. Even with the threat of electoral hostility they did none too well. After all, if they deserted those more favourable to Irish nationalistic Catholicism, Conservatism or abstention were the only alternatives short of revolt. Ironically enough, though, it was in Britain that a thorough integration between constitutionalism and Fenianism first took place. The absence there of Irish upper middle class and middle class leadership made it possible for Federalism to take on a particularly verdant 'Green' colour and the boundary line between loyalty to the Crown and loyalty to the democratic cause alone to become thoroughly blurred. When, in 1873, the Home Rule Confederation of Great Britain was founded, the model for what Parnell was to manufacture in Ireland itself became a fact.

Protestant Ulster under the Union was a good deal calmer than in the last quarter of the eighteenth century. Orangemen had occasional flings but, by and large, even in times of distress, disorder remained at a minimal level in comparison with the Catholic parts of the country. In the rural areas the tenantry were buttressed by the famous and much-coveted Ulster Tenant Right with its three F's and long tradition of give and take between landlord and peasant. In the towns the decline of some industries through British competition was often compensated for by the success in linen and the development of Belfast. Politically the Union assured Protestantism of all denominations. Yet all was not static and the radical spirit of the United Irishmen lingered on, above all among the Presbyterian tenant farmers. Social pressures to vote first Tory then Conservative were strong in the province, but with the secret ballot the Liberal cause made substantial progress. At the 1874 general election therefore, when most of Ireland veered away from Gladstone, the votes received by his supporters in the north shot up. One thing was certain, however, if the Liberal leader made political concessions to the Catholic majority, and that was a mass defection to those opposing him. Further agrarian reforms in the direction of tenant ownership were welcome in Ulster, but in the final analysis Protestant politics there ended as they began with the Union. Here was to be Parnell's greatest local obstacle during his reign as the 'Uncrowned King of Ireland'.

Backed by the same tradition which had motivated the stray outbreaks of Ribbonism in the country districts and Fenian activities throughout the United Kingdom just as much as it had O'Connell, the Federalists and the Irish

Independent Brigade—the tradition of feeling separate, whether in a patriotic or nationalistic manner—Isaac Butt set out to exploit the position at Westminster, which the backing a party of roughly sixty, returned in 1874 had given him, in the mildest possible way. The assembled ranks of British notables and the electorate behind them were to be impressed, so the theory went, with the loyalty, restraint and wisdom of the once rebellious island neighbour. Once they were partially cajoled, Butt hoped his own sweet reason would take them the rest of the way to the Federal solution and Irish 'Freedom'.

Into this situation came Parnell, inexperienced but perceptive, obscure but ambitious. From his presence in Parliament flowed the creation of the new Nationalist party incorporating the spirit of the Home Rule Confederation of Great Britain. In Ireland, the 'New Departure' of 1879, with its combination of the national and agrarian causes and its wooing of the most important sections of the Fenian support back into radical constitutional politics; then the Land League in its day to day work; then the National League and its adjuncts; and finally Parnell's own hard core—all represented aspects of the political skill of Charles Stewart Parnell. Over in the United States the Clan-na-Gael got used to the role of led rather than leader. Over in Britain the political game was played to force on success, or to survive for another bid for it. But in the end a good 'Big 'un' can smash a good 'Little 'un' and this hard fact Gladstone finally proved to Parnell. The career of the 'Uncrowned King' makes a splendid subject for those fascinated by the manifold facets of power, their advantages and disadvantages, and the consequences that spring therefrom. Few men had been so able at the power game as Parnell and few have operated in such a difficult field as the United Kingdom. A proper understanding of his place in history is therefore of high importance.

Biographical Notes

Not all the persons mentioned in the main text are included here. It has been assumed that men of the eminence of Kossuth, Hitler and Nehru need no introduction to anyone likely to read this book. On the other hand, there are those referred to whose fame has been more limited, or some details of whose lives are important to the full understanding of what follows. Hence the information printed below.

Biggar, Joseph Gillis (1828–1890).

After spending some time as a local nationalist politician in Belfast, where he plied in trade as a provision merchant, Biggar was elected Home Rule M.P. for the County Cavan in 1874 and kept the seat until his death. In 1870 he had joined Butt's Home Government Association, but five years later sought and obtained membership of the Irish Republican Brotherhood, better known as the Fenians. In the same year he began what became a famous obstruction policy in the

House of Commons, but remained firmly attached to the idea of a parliamentary Home Rule party, suffering expulsion from the Fenians in 1877 for his support of it and taking on the treasurership of the Land League at its foundation. After pursuing a course of strong opposition to Gladstone's Irish policy during 1880–1881, he was finally suspended from the Commons for disorderly conduct. His whole career came under the surveillance of the Parnell Commission.

Butt, Isaac (1813–1879).

Before founding the Home Government Association in 1870 and inaugurating the Irish Home Rule party Butt had had a long and distinguished career as an academic, magazine editor and barrister. A lifelong Protestant, he was before 1870 a stalwart Conservative, though from 1865 his faith in the Union as it stood had become severely undermined during work either defending or seeking amnesty for Fenian prisoners. From 1852–1865 he sat as a Conservative for Youghal, but in 1871 secured election as a Home Ruler in Limerick City. At Westminster he continued to lead the Home Rule party in the face of challenges from the Biggar-Parnell group right up to his death.

Croke, Thomas William (1824–1902).

After studying for the priesthood in France, Belgium and Italy Croke took his D.D. in 1847. For a time he served as professor of Ecclesiastical History at the Catholic University of Dublin and later as President of St. Colman's College, Fermoy.

Five years abroad as bishop of Auckland, New Zealand, were enough to secure him the stature for appointment to the archbishopric of Cashel in 1875. This post he filled until his death, but spiritual duties did not prevent his being a most active supporter of nationalistic and agrarian reform causes. He was prominent in the struggle against Parnell during 1890–1891.

Cullen, Paul (1803–1878).

Educated for the priesthood in Ireland and Italy, Cullen became Rector, first of the Irish College and then of the Propaganda College in Rome. The latter he saved from the Mazzinians during 1848–1849 by placing it under American protection. After three years as archbishop of Armagh he was transferred to Dublin, where he continued the campaign against extremist agitations over nationalism and the land begun in 1850. The highlight of his career as an archbishop was the receipt of a red hat in 1866, fourteen years after going to Dublin and two years after the foundation of the National Association with its moderate programme of ecclesiastical, agrarian and educational reform. He was an ardent enemy of the Fenians and constantly sought their discomfort and rout.

Devoy, John (1842–1928).

A prominent Fenian and accomplished journalist, Devoy went to the United States in 1871, having spent 1861–1866 as an active Irish revolutionary and five years in a British gaol. While in New York he first founded then edited the 'Irish Nation' (1881–1885) and the 'Gaelic American' (1903–1928). For the pre-1879 period he was a strong exponent of physical force politics, and reverted to such views in the post-Parnell years.

Grattan, Henry (1746–1820).

Three years after having been called to the bar Grattan entered the Irish Parliament for Charlemont in 1775. He was a constant agitator for Irish legislative independence and free trade between Britain and Ireland, achieving a great triumph in 1782 when his motion—in the form of an address to the Crown—demanding legislative independence was carried. His move was confirmed by statute and he became easily the most important member of the Irish Parliament in the period 1782–1800, reinforcing his position in 1790 by securing election for Dublin City. Catholic Emancipation and free trade were the causes foremost in his mind, and he was a vehement opponent of the Union in 1800, despite the bankruptcy of much of his creed proclaimed by the 1798 rebellion. As free trade was no longer a grievance under the Union, he concentrated on the Catholic question during his years as M.P. for Dublin City in the United Kingdom Parliament. His brand of Protestant liberalism wore rather thin in the face of O'Connell's movements, but death saved him from undue disappointment.

M'Cabe, Edward (1816–1885).

Educated for the priesthood at Maynooth, M'Cabe was a disciple of Cardinal Cullen's, and his assistant before succeeding him in the archbishopric of Dublin in 1879. Three years later the Pope created him a cardinal. In politics he is best known for his fierce denunciations of agrarian agitation and enmity to Parnell in the post-divorce suit period.

MacHale, John (1791–1881).

MacHale was both a pupil and teacher at Maynooth and did not visit Rome until 1831 after six years as coadjutor bishop of Killala. In 1834 he became archbishop of Tuam and at all times pursued as anti-English a course as his position allowed, supporting all nationalistic causes except where they clashed with the beliefs and interests of the Catholic Church. As early as 1801 he translated the Pentateuch into Irish, but not content with that did the same for portions of Moore's melodies and the works of Virgil. He sided with Parnell against Butt and favoured the Land League.

O'Shea, William Henry (1840–1905).

In 1867 O'Shea married Katharine Page Wood, later to become first the mistress and then the wife of Parnell. The O'Sheas met Parnell first in 1880 and Mrs. O'Shea very soon began a liaison with him. From 1882 she served as a go-between for her lover and Gladstone. Although O'Shea was almost certainly aware of his wife's misconduct, he did nothing, preferring to use her for his own pet schemes of self-advancement. As Home Rule M.P. for the County Clare (1880–1885) he had attempted to effect a compromise between the Liberal and Home Rule parties during the period 1882 to 1884. Much subsequent misunderstanding arose because of his failure to give accurate reports to one group of what the other one thought. Early in 1886 Parnell's influence gained him the Nationalist nomination for Galway City, but he never took the party pledge and in fact voted against the Home Rule Bill of 1886. Finally, for reasons which are not altogether clear, he at last cited Parnell as co-respondent in a divorce suit against his wife and obtained his freedom in 1890. Subsequently Parnell and Katherine O'Shea got married. Very probably O'Shea had held off for so long because of hopes of monetary gain and when these were disappointed felt he could proceed. Nevertheless, the possibility of politics being at least a concomitant motive cannot be entirely discounted. Certainly they were not the prime one, otherwise action could and would have been taken long before 1889.

Shaw, William (1823–1895).

At one time a Congregationalist minister and in charge of a church in Cork, Shaw subsequently took up banking and entered Parliament as M.P. first for Bandon (1868–1874) and then for the County Cork (1874–1885). He was a Liberal of strong Home Rule sympathies and succeeded Butt as chairman of the Home Rule party from 1879 to 1880. After being displaced by Parnell he left the Home Rule ranks and supported Gladstone. Five years later he was declared bankrupt.

Tone, Theobald Wolfe, (1763–1798).

Following a truly chaotic and undisciplined early career, Tone was called to the bar in 1789 and soon embarked upon a campaign in favour of Irish independence, seeking to unite

Catholics, Presbyterians and other Protestant nonconformists against the government in Dublin and its London controllers. A prominent figure in the United Irishmen, he became involved with a French spy, but was permitted to leave Ireland for the United States in 1795. The next year, however, he voyaged to Paris and there assisted in French schemes for the invasion of Ireland. Ultimately he sailed to Ireland in 1798 with a small French expedition intended to assist general rebellion and was captured by the authorities. Rather than be refused a soldier's death he committed suicide. His writings lived on, though, and played an interesting part in keeping the concept of Irish nationality alive in the minds of a people alienated from their rulers at almost all levels.

1 Irish Nationalism, the Continent and the Anglo-American Tradition

Irish patriotism and nationalism have been viewed too exclusively in an Anglo-American context. The fault is understandable enough. England had long dominated Ireland and imposed fundamental political, social and economic changes upon her. A ruling class imported or largely assimilated to foreign standards, a colonial class systematically settled in important areas, a religion and language strongly backed from outside—all drew the country into the conqueror's orbit. When neglect and ill-treatment provoked resentment against authority in London, the movements for greater autonomy were led by the appointed agents of the oppressor. Geography and economics played havoc with traditional ties and produced a fresh breed of Irish 'patriots'. So low had the 'native' Catholic race fallen that their contribution to the upsurge leading to the establishment of what is called Grattan's Parliament in 1782 was extremely slight. But the rôle of grateful recipient soon changed to one of national self-assertion among certain elements of a partially emancipated majority. Nevertheless, their leaders and substantial numbers of the Protestant colonial class tended to draw their inspiration from across the Atlantic, where men of a very similar kind had lately thrown off British control and set up a republic. Washington and his like made possible not only the moderate and essentially loyal Grattanite changes, but stimulated a thorough-going republican Irish nationalism, which was ultimately to triumph in the twentieth century. Religious animosity beggared it in 1798 and long continued to do so. The colonial class was to provide the British with their strongest card in the Irish game by the end of the nineteenth century. It valued its Protestantism above its republicanism and saw in the British Crown a protection against the Catholic Church and a 'native' majority devoted to its faith. During the period from the legislative Union of Britain and Ireland in 1800 until the end of the 1850's, the main initiatives in Irish politics lay with those like O'Connell, who valued constitutionalism and were patriots rather than nationalists, royalists rather than republicans, Grattanites rather than revolutionaries. It seemed quite natural to accept them as part of the Anglo-Saxon scene. Underneath the surface all the time, and on the surface some of the time, the extreme revolutionary party existed as both a supplement and dangerous rival to the moderate cause. In the 1860's most of it crystallized around the Fenian movement, an organization owing much of its force to Irish settlers in the United States. The trans-atlantic link once remade was never again completely broken. Butt's constitutional Home Rule movement began as part of the O'Connell type tradition, yet rapidly drifted into something more ambitious during the course of the 1870's. And this is where the nationalism of our subject and the party he built up came in. American money enabled him to make the most of vast popular support. British traditions and allies gave him enormous openings. His methods and their effectiveness were undeniably different from those of others who had trodden the parliamentary path. Viewed in an Anglo-American context alone, however, something of his significance is lost. Of course, Parnell and his party were a part, indeed an important part, of the late nineteenth-century English-speaking world. Even so, within it they were then unique. Only outside it was anything like them to be found. The direct action party had been largely absorbed into the constitutionalist cause. Why that was can only be understood by subjecting both the new leader and the groups he welded into the Irish Nationalist party to a thorough analysis. In making it the parallel developments on the continent provide some useful analogies—analogies pointing to something of a common heritage.

France as well as the United States and the British left, had given considerable impetus to Irish self-esteem. The Union itself was due in part to the revolutionary nationalist activity of Paris and its allies. Wolfe Tone looked to them more immediately than to any 'New World' inspiration. The international influence of the Catholic Church and the contact between O'Connell and constitutionalist liberal Catholics in France were also of prime importance. Ireland was not isolated from non-English influences by her geographical position and political status. The 'Liberator' may have been a Benthamite, but he was also the leader of what amounted to the first formidable Christian Democratic movement. Then too, in 1848 the leftmost of the Irish constitutionalists went

33

over to violence and, though lacking a grassroots following of any size, rose in abortive rebellion. They formed part of the Young Ireland movement, the very title of which was an indication of continental inspiration. Mazzini, Young Italy and the modern nationalist ideal were gods in their pantheon. Fenianism may have had its United States side, but in some ways that was the superficial aspect of the story. Irish America was not the United States. Whereas comparative remoteness, a long period of independence and tolerably friendly relations with the outside world had taken some of the bitterness out of the usual degree of national self-assertiveness prevalent in that country, the Irish immigrants were looking very much more to the past. They had two nationalisms—American and Irish. The latter they indulged in ways out of keeping with the ordinary American traditions. Fenianism owed more to Mazzini and Young Ireland than to the 'Founding Fathers'. Lalor's land reform notions were abandoned, yet much of the motive power behind the movement sprang from agrarian miseries. Though without the social programme of the men of 1848, Fenianism was Young Ireland's violent wing writ large. The grassroots had come at last. But during the period of unmitigated rejection of constitutionalism in Fenian circles Catholic influence was cast furiously in a contrary direction. Whether in the form of the ultramontanism of Cardinal Cullen, or the quasi-Gallicanism of Archbishop MacHale following in the tradition of O'Connell, something essentially outside of the accepted Anglo-American world again made the pace in an important sphere of Irish politics. Butt initially drew some Fenian support for his Home Rule movement, only to lose it as his ineffective strategy became plain. Support from official Catholic sources was slower in coming, but even slower to go. By the time of Butt's death, Catholic grass roots were the only ones he had. Parnell welded together the diverse elements of realistic Irish nationalism in quite a short time. Both the constitutionalist and revolutionary groups had traditions drawn both from inside and outside the Anglo-American world. Their new leader shared this mixture of background. Its importance can be seen from the salient features of his career. Nothing, however, should be allowed to obscure the fact that most Fenians were devout Catholics and many Catholic priests were far from unsympathetic to Fenianism. The major struggle in Ireland when Parnell was to the fore, between 1874 and 1891, was between a Catholic majority, bursting with economic grievances and enamoured of a full-blown modern Irish nationalism, and a Protestant minority, economically better off and very content to merge its Irishness, such as it was, into a wider British nationalism. Despite what the nationalist propagandists said and say, Ireland the island was not Ireland the nation. That was made up of the majority. Nevertheless, the myth of national unity was persisted in by Parnell, a Protestant and a landlord, just as it had been by those putting old-fashioned patriotism and modern nationalism first in the preceding decades. Grattan, O'Connell, Young Ireland, the Fenians and Butt had all talked of Ireland the *nation*. Only the first had been at all justified, and then merely because of a transitory phase when all Irishmen had common grievances to work off against Britain. In the last analysis the crucial factor behind the career of Parnell was the motive power upon which he was able to draw —the motive power of majority discontent. The masterly handling of the differing traditions simply maximised its effect.

Parnell has received a great deal of attention from historians of late. By and large their researches and arguments have been of a high quality. First, in 1949, came Professor T. W. Moody's essay on 'The New Departure in Irish Politics, 1878–9'.[1] Some eight years later C. C. O'Brien brought out 'Parnell and his Party, 1880–90', only to be followed in 1959 and 1960 by Professor F. S. L. Lyons with an essay: 'The Economic Ideas of Parnell',[2] and a book: 'The Fall of Parnell, 1890–91'. Last year David Thornley's 'Isaac Butt and Home Rule' offered fresh information on the earlier years of the Parnellite movement and repeated the arguments about the obstructive tactics of the Biggar-Parnell 'ginger group' in the House of Commons previously presented in 'Irish Historical Studies'. Notable among short pieces on Parnell and his party were C. H. D. Howard's 'The Parnell Manifesto of 21 November, 1885, and the Schools Question'[3] of 1947 and Professor Lyons's pamphlet 'Parnell' of 1963.[4] On the other side of the Atlantic Emmet Larkin published an article on 'The Roman Catholic Hierarchy and the Fall of Parnell' in 1961[5] and followed it up two years later with another entitled: 'Mounting the Counter-Attack: The Roman

[1] In *Essays in British and Irish History in Honour of James Eadie Todd* (London, 1949).

[2] In *Historical Studies*, II (Papers read to the Third Conference of Irish Historians), edited by Michael Roberts (Cambridge, 1959).

[3] In the *English Historical Review*, 1947.

[4] Irish History Series No. 3. (Published for the Dublin Historical Association, Dublin, 1963).

[5] In *Victorian Studies*, 1961.

Catholic Hierarchy and the Destruction of Parnellism'.[6]
All without exception shy away to some extent from what
C. C. O'Brien terms the 'ultimate motives' behind Parnell's
political activities, though it is only fair to add that Professor
Lyons offends least in this regard. Most of them have written
about the middle and last years of the great man's career. This
made an avoidance of a full-scale attempt to define what made
him 'tick' relatively easy. A man operating 'in medias res' is
interesting to observe, exploiting changes in the political
context to his advantage, achieving substantial successes in
building up influence, and falling to destruction through
human frailty. But what is the good of studying tactics, or
even short term strategy, without having come to some conclusions, albeit negative ones, about the overall preoccupations
of that man? To the plea that caution necessitated an almost
general reticence it may be answered that there is no want of
evidence about the deeds of Parnell, nor is the absence of
some equivalent of 'Mein Kampf' really any bar to taking the
plunge. Because much of the evidence is conflicting the
historian has a hard task, but a hard task is not necessarily an
impossible one, and personal testaments, above all those
intended for publication, are often deliberately misleading and
merely put yet another stumbling block in the way of those
probing for the full and accurate explanation of events. Had
more attention been paid to Parnell's formative years and the
first bouts in politics, the evaluation of long as opposed to
short-term aims would surely have been less difficult to make?
R. Barry O'Brien produced in 1899 what is undeniably an
able biography. On the subject of fundamental aims and

[6] In the *Review of Politics*, 1963

objects he plunges in regardless. Given the irritating, though understandable, modern habit of dealing only with the full-blown and grown politician, his account of the pre-'New Departure' Parnell has a particular value. Parnellite affiliations and the nearness of the publication date to the heart-rending controversy surrounding the split in the Irish Nationalist party in no way invalidate the basic information used in the text. To that part coping with the earlier years the work of Professor Lyons serves rather as a supplement than as a refutation. Other older writings on the subject do not, in general, measure up to the O'Brien biography, whether for the early, middle, or late periods. On the early one no modern writer has displaced it. The author knew his subject personally and has never been shown to be anything but an honest man. As a foundation for discussion his overall performance is therefore worthy of serious consideration.

2   *Parnell Revealed*

There were four main stages in Parnell's political life. The first ended with his being elected chairman of the Irish Home Rule parliamentary party in 1880; the second with Gladstone's adoption of the principle of Irish Home Rule in 1885; the third with the publication of Gladstone's condemnatory letter in 1890; and the last with his death in 1891. During the rise to and consolidation of power in the first three of these stages, circumstances seemed geared to secure his success. Brilliant leadership appeared to have been given its head. At the end of 1890 the fates proved too much for him. Some have regarded his conduct as lacking judgment after Gladstone pronounced against him. There is much to be said against this. Making the best of a bad job acquired almost a new dimension in his hands. That Parnell was an extraordinary man can safely be assumed. However much fortune first made then marred him, his own contribution to moulding events was quite remarkable. What sort of man he was and what exactly he sought to achieve are less easily explained. 'Superficially', says C. C. O'Brien, 'there was a paradox in the rise of a Protestant landlord to the leadership of a Catholic people in its fight against landlordism.'[1] Yes indeed, but why there was not a paradox at a profounder level we are not told. His family was undoubtedly part of the Protestant 'Ascendancy' as regards social and religious alignments, yet it had never regarded the Union of 1800 as anything but a vastly unwelcome bugbear. It had championed Catholic Emancipation and never been attached to any political cause to the right of a progressive Liberalism. Its tenants had reason to be grateful for the benevolent and scrupulous treatment they received. Within the walls of the house at Avondale, near Rathdrum in County Wicklow, the words 'justice' and 'liberty' had a very real meaning. Into this atmosphere Parnell's father brought a bride for whom its traditions were highly congenial. She was an American—the daughter of a Commodore in the United States navy, who had seen service against the British in the war of 1812–14. In 1846—a dread year in Irish history—her son Charles Stewart Parnell was born. As a boy he was delicate, sensitive and impossible with those he disliked. A strong desire to prevail characterized most of his actions, though he soon demonstrated his belief in doing justice and helping the weak and unfortunate. Here was a benevolent despot in the making. At school and university in England he made no real mark, except as an insubordinate and aggressive nuisance. England, on the other hand, made a deep impression on him. He disliked it intensely, partly no doubt because some of the citizens had attempted to bring him to heel from time to time in their educational establishments, partly because of the

[1] C. C. O'Brien, *Parnell and his Party, 1880–1890* (Oxford, 1957), p. 6.

attitude shown towards him as an Irish visitor. Comments to his brother John, made while at Magdalene College, Cambridge, reveal the future Nationalist leader as someone thinking of himself primarily as an Irishman and someone already convinced that the best method of dealing with the English was to 'stand up to them'.[2] R. Barry O'Brien saw Parnell as having been stuffed full of anti-English sentiment by a formidable and fanatically inclined American mother. She was said to have been a 'regular rebel'.[3] The chances are that this was so, for despite what Professor Lyons stresses about her having attended the Viceregal court and entertained British officers,[4] her anti-British inclinations are beyond doubt. How else could she have sympathized with the Fenians to the extent she did? Butt might have wanted them amnestied. She said she wanted them to rule and send the English back where they 'belonged'. The indignation later voiced by T. M. Healy against the English assumption that God had given their race a permanent lease of the universe she shared to the full. Why should the English alone be allowed to be nationalists? Of course, the stridency of her pronouncements may have exceeded her readiness for change and in any case her son was no empty cask into which propaganda could be poured like a liquid. Still, we know that Parnell was very amenable to those for whom he cared, however hostile he showed himself to others he disliked. His passion for home life suggests his relationship with his mother must have been

[2] R. Barry O'Brien, *The Life of Charles Stewart Parnell* (London, 1899), Vol I, p. 41.
[3] R. Barry O'Brien, op. cit., p. 39.
[4] F. S. L. Lyons, *The Fall of Parnell* (London, 1960), p. 4.

close. But whether this notion is right or wrong added influences were at work on him in Ireland long before he darkened the doors of Cambridge and encountered a more sophisticated brand of English arrogance than he had met at school. Wicklow had been the scene of revolution in 1798. Many of the older men and women Parnell met in his youth were still full of what had happened. History in Ireland had then as often now the compelling quality of current affairs. In the very year when he was born Ireland had been ravaged by famine. The political, social, and economic influence of the landlord class of which he was a member aroused chronic discontent all around him. A sensitive young man, reared in such a household was quite likely to let sympathy with the underdog accentuate any dislike he may have had for 'Castle' government and British authority. At the time he entered the House of Commons, in 1875, his interests in Irish difficulties were general. The least vague of his aims were the political. Justice and liberty alike, he thought, dictated the need for Irish self-government. But if he was something of a romantic, he was also a stark realist on how to go about things. Fenianism meant business, therefore Fenianism was worthwhile. The secret ballot would deprive landlords of certain kinds of power, therefore it provided an opening for sending back tougher representatives to Westminster. Sentiment clouded his initial assessments of both matters, yet if his premises were false, his reasoning from them was not. British strength was overwhelming. Standing up to it would therefore require overwhelming effort. The practical nationalist had to be an unscrupulous one. All openings had to be exploited. This capacity for grasping essentials was to take Parnell far. The capacity to work from a highly emotional position with striking practical skill was to take him even further. Construction of an effective Irish Nationalist party brought him to abandon amelioration policies for the land and to embrace root and branch reform. Being something of a scientist made it easier, even for a 'political genius' like him, to appreciate the need to harness energy. The campaign he undertook inevitably involved using this energy. Here his genius was taxed to the uttermost, for when an extremist plays with moderation to win a power game he has to have supreme control over his forces. This he had during the first three stages defined above. Circumstances had worked on him to make the Irish nationalist, circumstances then worked more to define the policy that went with it. Because he was quick to see how each component of the power structure existing at any given point was made, and grasped how best to use them all to his own advantage a dual process was begun. So much so that circumstances appeared to work for him.

We have then a man whose emotional force was powerful enough to sustain the extraordinary practical side of his nature. This combination applied in both public and private spheres; in the regions of love and hate; and in whatever environment he happened to find himself. It has often been argued that Parnell was past master at keeping his emotions under control. But what real evidence is there for this? The truth is that he was a man of gigantic emotions which carried him through complicated situations with comparative ease. The physical price he paid for carrying such heavy guns was great and in ill-health many have seen the results of keeping himself in check. It seems more plausible, however, given the sum total of what we know about him, to argue that it was experiencing such vast currents of emotional electricity that tired him out and made him seek long periods of repose. Another school of thought has seen in him a man cast in a Lenin-like mould. This is even further wide of the mark. Coldness in manner did not signify coldness in nature, and, what is more, someone so loving on one side could never have been unfeeling and fishlike on the other. Emotional self-indulgence sticks out a mile in the years before he entered politics. At home, school, university and in the social life of County Wicklow, where he became High Sheriff, the way he behaved was highly emotional. Fenianism and the tragic affair of the Manchester 'Martyrs' reinforced his already active hatred of England and its government in Ireland. Enthusiasm pushed him into the rough and tumble of electioneering in the midst of the 1874 general election campaign and zest for victory in the Home Rule battle just ran away with him. What C. C. O'Brien rightly terms his 'prudence and daring, firmness and flexibility, farsightedness and tactical sense'[5] were the result of his being able to infuse his emotional experiences with direction and purpose. Intelligence dictated the priority he gave to basic matters. Highly emotional people can indulge their feelings without lapsing into errors of judgment in their battles with opponents, or descending to the rantings and ravings of a Hitler or Mussolini. We have seen that Parnell was wayward with those he disliked. Did this change after he became an M.P.? We know it did not and that he out-Biggared Biggar, a process which first made his reputation as a Nationalist politician. 'Standing up to the English'

[5] C. C. O'Brien, op. cit., p. 7.

by flogging what most M.P.'s sincerely wished was a dead horse, whether it is viewed as straightforward obstructionist devilry, or a legitimate maximum use of genuine arguments,[6] was a most enjoyable game. Emotional satisfaction was to be had from it in plenty. As the need to galvanize all sections of nationalist opinion into united action for realizing his pet notion of an independent Irish legislature became increasingly apparent, his feelings overcame any class scruples he may have had. Davitt was an accurate and truthful man. His view that Parnell was out for as much independence as he could get by the end of the 1870's cannot anyway be lightly dismissed. The nature of the young aristocrat's approach to his new tasks support it up to the hilt. High passion worked for the maximum demand and unerring practicality for an acceptance of any instalment promised by the despicable British. The openings for such a leader were startlingly good between 1875 and 1880. In a manner of speaking he was the 'Messiah' for whom the Catholic masses had long been waiting. In the second phase he mastered the centrifugal extravagances of the Land League to an extent Butt would never have dreamed of and gradually the Catholic hierarchy took steps towards the band-wagon. When they lifted up their skirts and jumped upon it he remained the

---

[6] For a discussion of the problem see D. Thornley, 'The Irish Home Rule Party and Parliamentary Obstruction, 1874–1887', Historical Revision: XI, *Irish Historical Studies*, 1960. More on the subject is to be found in the same author's *Isaac Butt and Home Rule* (London, 1964), Chapter 12. Naturally, Parnell and Biggar sometimes took the business before the House of Commons seriously. Even so, they saw to it that anything was turned against the 'English' whenever possible. A legitimate argument could be unduly prolonged just as an unwarranted one could be begun.

unchallenged driver. Many have seen in the adhesion of the Catholic priests proof of a rightward trend in Parnell's policy. Yet it was surely nothing but a matter of tactics. The inner delight of the hope of ultimate success satisfied his emotions. Tactics may have changed from time to time between his becoming *de jure* as well as *de facto* leader and the 1885 general election, but there is nothing really to show that the position of the late seventies had been abandoned. Historians have tended to confuse methods with aims in dealing with the Irish question. Words like 'conservative', 'extremist', 'moderate' and 'revolutionary' have all tended to become hopelessly misused. To those accustomed to the methods of modern subversion deeds are not decisive in judging a man in the way they are to others, unversed in the ways of the undemocratic politicians. For Parnell, working on a day to day basis was attractive. He liked the process of laying his traps. Did Brer Fox have to exercise all that much self-control as he watched potential victims approach his tar-baby? Naturally, there was, as C. C. O'Brien claims, an inordinate amount of duplicity used in holding the new Nationalist party together and running it successfully as part of United Kingdom politics.[7] Even so, was not the duplicity at the expense of the fringes? Were not its real victims the violence 'boys' of the left and the quavering hierarchs and their minions on the right? The former would have rejected interim measures and started what they could not finish, discrediting the whole Nationalist cause in the process. The latter would have been even keener than many of them were in any case to dilute the Home Rule brew with the 'holy

[7] C. C. O'Brien, op. cit., p. 350.

water' of devolution schemes. After Gladstone took up Home
Rule, in phase three, the question was more one of holding
hard than advancing further. But then the party had been
shaped into a modern nationalist organization, representing
the overwhelming proportion of Catholic Ireland and a few
Protestants of an unusual turn of mind. Fighting was directed
against the Unionist government of Lord Salisbury and its
Irish administration. As before, coercion in Ireland and new
procedure rules in the House of Commons were stimulants to
national self-assertion as well as practical curbs upon its wilder
aspects. For a man with Parnell's emotional make-up this
great battle within sight of the partially 'Celestial City' of
Home Rule was a great thrill. The demands it made upon his
skill in no way detracted from its concordance with his basic
political desires. Once the fall began virtually everyone agrees
that Parnell's emotions burst forth. Yet were his general
political abilities exercised to no purpose because of that?
Within the limits set him by his enemies he not only fought,
but fought with resource and courage. As always, his basic
premiss, that he alone was leader of the Irish nation, was
highly emotional and the actions that hinged upon it were
both logical and imaginative. The mixture was as before.
Human beings remain essentially the same throughout their
lives. Parnell was to die young. Throughout the comparatively
short period of sixteen years that he spent in politics he was
under serious stress of one kind and another. For almost
the whole period of his leadership Mrs. O'Shea was an inti-
mate companion. What makes the last phase appear so much
more emotional is the tragedy of failure after so much achieved
and the internecine warfare amongst the Nationalists. Few

things could have been more of a strain than the Special Commission sessions until the exposure of Pigott in February 1889. Nevertheless, the rows in Committee Room 15 and throughout the three crucial Parnellite versus anti-Parnellite by-elections seem infinitely worse. Complete innocence may have been a comfort to a man of Parnell's pride and dignity during what amounted to an indirect state trial, but guilt would not appear to have been among his worries as failure moved in upon him. He never accepted the moral code of his detractors and claimed the valid charge of adultery laid at his door was as nothing in face of honourable conduct towards the allegedly indignant husband. The emotional temperature at which he worked in the months before his death might have been higher had he really had a deep emotional attachment to the leading anti-Parnellites. On the whole he had not. Only W. O'Brien enjoyed his genuine affection and the mode of his defection was such as to leave as little bitterness as it was possible to leave in that bitter affair. Those he loved remained the most select of bands. One, first his mistress, then his wife, he loved above all else. Even to think of Lenin in the context of *in principio mulier est hominis confusio* is ludicrous in the extreme. For the 'uncrowned king of Ireland' the tag is apposite to a degree.

Another puzzling element in the Parnell saga is the attitude he had towards the Irish Catholic masses as people. As a cause, as something to strive for, they were close to his heart. But, as we have seen, those individuals who actually evoked affection were few and far between. Most strange of all in some ways is that just after being elected leader of a modern nationalist party he should rush into making an English-

woman of ruling class background his mistress. It is hard not
to believe that in essentials his leadership of the 'popular'
side in Ireland was a supreme piece of patronage. Born a
leader in a class of leaders his approach was arrogant yet
merciful. Added to which, he was preeminently fastidious and
contemptuous of vulgarity. From the very beginning he
despised many of his lieutenants for their inferior ability,
petty jealousies, susceptibility to upper class influence wielded
at Westminster and lack of good breeding. For him the end of
the 'Ascendancy' would not mean Ireland would necessarily
become a shopocracy. To be sure the party had to be broad
based, and, of course, the poorer classes had powerful reasons
for proving loyal servants of the Nationalist party. Nevertheless, for its leader the party was not as other parties. It was a
movement to put him in charge of the initiative in United
Kingdom politics so that Ireland might have an Irish government. What sort of government would result was not clear.
Asquith was right to insist that Parnell was no democrat.
Perhaps the régime he envisaged in his moments of greatest
optimism had more in common with that of Nkrumah's Ghana
than the present day Irish Republic. Circumstances demanded a
dictator and Parnell was one. His social background, manner
and appearance all militated in his favour, as did Gladstone's in
a different way in Britain. One on top of the social ladder has
experience and prestige denied to the parvenu, however great
his innate intellectual and political abilities. T. M. Healy and
Joseph Chamberlain were to learn this truth the hard way.

If all this be true, Mrs. O'Shea becomes less of an enigma.
Being the man he was, Parnell could only have fallen in love
with someone of sensitivity, imagination, and good manners,

capable of great kindness and loyalty to his person and opinions. This paragon in other words had to belong to his private world and be willing to join his public one in spirit at least. Socially the English and Anglo-Irish upper-crusts shared a common culture. His choosing one of the oppressors was therefore not ruled out on non-political grounds and Mrs. O'Shea put love before politics. Because of the rôle she played in negotiating with Gladstone and the importance she rightly placed on capturing the British Liberals for the Home Rule cause some have regarded her as an English viper in the nest. This is extremely difficult to square with the argument that in the last phase she was keeping Parnell in an unreasonable frame of mind and was the prime motive force behind his refusal to agree to a temporary retirement. *La donna e mobile,* but such a *volte face* seems highly unlikely. Both activities point to her doing what Parnell wanted most at each particular period.

Despite all the comment excited by Parnell's being a Protestant and landlord in charge of a Catholic mass movement intent upon taking over the land, his position was far from singular when viewed in the wider context of British and world history. In the Gladstonian Liberal party a largely aristocratic and Anglican leadership was to preside over numerous reforms directed towards the reduction of the power and privileges of their class and their church. Hyndman and Cunninghame-Graham, William Morris and the Fabians, judged by British standards, had little more in common with the workmen they championed than Parnell with the peasants of County Mayo. Other nationalist leaders on the continent often displayed a certain separateness from their followers.

Cultural differences divided Cavour from the bulk of the classes in the Italian Risorgimento. His prime language was French and he regaled the Piedmontese parliament with long speeches in it. Kossuth was Hungarian by adoption. Both his parents were Slovak. It was as though T. M. Healy had become Grand Master of the Orangemen. Pilsudski had Lithuanian origins, yet pushed Polish nationalism to extremes. European Socialist leaders were often, like Blum, drawn from outside the working classes. Neither Lenin—the son of a bureaucrat promoted into the aristocracy—nor Trotsky—son of a Jewish Kulak—sprang from the proletariat they purported to place in power. In the wider world the anti-colonialist struggle, with which the nationalism of the dis-contented European communities had so much in common, produced numerous leaders, who, as in Parnell's case, man-aged to combine nationalism with a left-wing brand of domestic programme. The fact that a Brahmin from a rich home should advocate the creation of equality before the law in a predominantly lay state for all Indians, Untouchables and Moslems included, tends to reduce the element of the spectac-ular associated in most minds with Parnell. The profundity of religious, class and community differences in India far ex-ceeded that in Ireland. The careers of Nehru and his like marked a degree of adventure not reached by Parnell.

Looked at over a long period, Irish affairs were like a modern colonialist problem played in slow motion. So too, in some respects, were nationalist movements amongst con-tinental peoples such as the Croats, Czechs, Hungarians, Poles, Slovaks and Slovenes. English then British conquest and administration transformed Ireland from a geographical expression with a loose sense of oneness into a unit the indigenous population of which regarded as the rightful recipient of its emotional loyalty. Unfortunately for this population, extraneous elements introduced by conquest stood in the way of any claim that Ireland was inhabited exclusively by an Irish race. Nor did events work to absorb the original population into the British type traditions to an extent sufficient to destroy the potent feeling of separateness already existing before the attainment of true unity. Indeed, the Catholic Church drew great strength from its bad relations with the overwhelming proportion of the British peoples and the British government in pre-toleration times. Under the Grattan régime it looked for a time as though some form of what might be termed state nationalism might emerge, but 1798 killed all hopes of that and the Union transferred the whole question into the much wider context of the United Kingdom. Ireland then became the battleground of Irish versus British nationality. Irish nationalism was the nationalism of a particular section of the community. In India, the Moslems had been introduced by pre-British conquests. Within the state machine created under the British, unity amongst the nationalistic elements was short-lived. Fear of Hinduism operated upon the Moslems much as fear of Catholicism had upon the Presbyterian Republicans of Ulster, except that differences of geography and relationship with the British made partition and independence rather than Union with the United Kingdom the only feasible policy to pursue. Indian Congress party nationalism therefor became for all intents and purposes a Hindu community party, although it had its 'Protestant Home Rulers' in the persons of some individual Moslems for whom the concept of a united India had an over-riding attraction. State nationalism had created English (then British) and French national feeling. Varying sections of the territory under one ruler had become nation states. Self-ruling nuclei had augmented nationalisms such as the German, Greek, Italian, Roumanian and Serbian. The Austrian state machine in the nineteenth century found itself unable to sweep away the nationalistic stirring amongst peoples other than the Austrian Germans and groups closely tied to them. As with the Irish Catholics, so with some of these groups, the nationalism often had the appearance of the upsurge of a community. Religion was not commonly a distinguishing factor, but class and race often went together. At first, the Habsburgs found themselves surrounded by a gaggle of Grattans, then by one of O'Connells, and then by one of Parnells. Ultimately, movements of the Sinn Fein variety occasionally sprang up, especially in the South Slav areas. The Hungarians achieved far more in this game before the Austrian Empire collapsed than anyone else. From 1867 they managed to control what had historically been the territory of the Hungarian Crown and attempt its thoroughgoing Magyarization. The distribution of power inside the Habsburg lands allowed them to attempt what Parnell and Nehru wanted so badly. Their failure to carry the process to a successful conclusion is hardly surprising, but the *fons et origo* of their strength lay largely in the possession of something Parnell and many of the other continental movements lacked. All classes of Hungarians supported the grand bid for independence. Kossuth and Tisza actually had what Young Ireland had often dreamed of—the magnate and the peasant under the same banner. Nehru enjoyed the same advantage. But being trapped in the United

Kingdom state machine Irish nationalism was subject to certain types of atrophy. When the 'popular' side was led by O'Connell richer Catholics in the middle class often supported its aims and activities. Note the words 'middle class'— most aristocratic Catholics had soon subsided into a quietist variety of Unionism. As time passed and the content of nationalistic programmes tended to include an increasing number of social reforms, many of them extremely radical in tendency, there took place an attrition of support among the better off sections of the Catholic community, especially that part of it connected with the ownership of land. Things of the pocket played havoc with the sense of national indignation so many of them had felt when the land was securely under their feet. Men who had actually sat as Home Rule M.P.'s of the Butt-Shaw connection as late as 1880 were Liberal Unionists by the summer of 1886. How sincere their nationalistic tendencies had ever been is, of course, open to question. The fact remains, however, that they took a firm stand against nationalism with an extreme radical content, and all too often Irish affairs have been written about and discussed as though there was an essential sameness between the leaders and supporters of self-assertive movements founded on the Catholic masses.

That O'Connell differed from Grattan is taken for granted, but if that, why is O'Connell spoken of as a nationalist as if his attitude to the Union had been on a par with the Sinn Feiners? Words simply become meaningless if used in that way. Why too, is so much stress put on methods as opposed to policies? From some accounts anyone would think the prime differences between Butt and Parnell stemmed from matters of organization and tactics. A horrible sameness has so obtruded itself into history as to make the words 'Irish leader' conjure up some curious figure compounding the basic beliefs of O'Connell, Butt, Parnell and De Valera and yet possessed of no uniform means of political action. Parnell's Irish nationalism was a distinct thing. To write, as Professor Moody does, of 'O'Connell and the men of 1848 . . . as the pioneers, for the nineteenth century, of the moral-force and the physical force schools of nationalism respectively', without at the same time stressing that there were frequent and powerful cross-currents between the two sides in the ideological field is very misleading.[8] Why the term 'modern nationalism' has been used above in connection with Parnell is because the differences of degree between O'Connell, Butt and Parnell were such as almost to amount to those of kind. This applies with particular force to the things separating Parnell from the other two. All three would have agreed with Hitler's words; 'I do not myself believe that any nation (i.e. state) not rooted in the people, born of the people and desired by the people, can in the long run maintain itself.' But, taking the political sphere alone, neither of the earlier leaders could be said to have been avowed nationalists in the sense that the word is now understood. Certainly, O'Connell was anathema to countless Anglo-Irish Whigs and Liberals on a variety of grounds. Some dreaded him as a Catholic and demagogue advocating 'popular' politics, others hated either the religious or political aspect alone. Nevertheless, O'Connell's cosmopolitanism

[8] T. W. Moody, 'The New Departure in Irish Politics, 1878–1879', in *Essays in British and Irish History in Honour of James Eadie Todd*, p. 306.

went infinitely further than Parnell's and he was deeply impressed with the parliamentary system of government at Westminster and the potential advantage of a true Union. He therefore wavered somewhat in his quest for Repeal and flirted with the Federal notion later espoused by Butt. Feeling from below kept him in line, but it is hard to see him as anything but a patriot of patriots whose keen practical sense took him into tough policies because 'standing up to the British' paid off. Young Ireland quarrelled with him precisely because he was not a convinced nationalist. In his heart he really wanted what Herzl had initially set out to achieve for the Jews—fair integration. Paradoxically enough, his deep Catholicism did not prove a stumbling block to his liberalism. He was attached to it as a faith rather than as a political badge. Butt was never properly nationalistic and his patriotism lacked the emotional content of O'Connell's. He was the far-seeing Conservative questing for justice and utility and trying simultaneously to serve the best interests of the United Kingdom by seeking the reconciliation of Britain and Ireland through Home Rule. But the crucial point is not the convictions of these two leaders, but the motive force which sustained their activities. The basic sense of nationalism among the Catholic masses, including, needless to say, economic and social grievances, gave the Repeal and Buttite Home Rule movements health and strength. As politics became more 'popular' in fact as well as in name the actual influence exercised by the lower classes necessarily increased and the true nature of their dearest wishes became crystal clear. Repeal and Buttite politics became too moderate. Fenianism embodied much better than had Young Ireland the essence of mass Irish nationalism. Parnell made it adopt a means of operating fitted to the circumstances of the United Kingdom. Parnell rose higher above the people than O'Connell and vastly higher than Butt, yet he was much nearer to it. O'Connell had a large heart, but it sometimes beat out a United Kingdom theme. In choosing a nominal constitutionalism as the basis for operations Parnell just did what intelligent nationalist leaders in similar situations had done, did and were to do. Italy had won her independence on the battlefield, but not alone. Despite Irish America, Parnell saw he was alone. There could be no question of *Irlanda fara da se* by force. Prussia had created German unity by military might. Ireland possessed no military might. For the small peoples brain rather than brawn must always be the order of the day. Parnell had the ability to persuade a nation keen on a fight to make it one primarily of words and votes. Butt's men had spoken of fighting with ballot boxes not bullets. Parnell did just this and demonstrated the ballot box had a value as an offensive weapon it was not commonly supposed to possess. But then, he had fitted to it several revolutionary accessories.

3 The Route to the Irish Nationalist Leadership

An examination of the four stages of his career bears out the appraisals of his character and performance set out above. It was ironic that his original standing with the forces of Irish nationalism should have arisen from performances as a member of the Westminster parliament—a body neither he nor they held in anything but contempt. The prelude to fame was odd in the extreme. Butt's Home Rule movement was the obvious vehicle for anyone eager to enter the House of Commons on the Irish 'popular' side in 1874 to use. Respectable social affiliations and the means to bear the cost of an election were recommendations to the so-called drivers of that vehicle. Nevertheless, acceptance of Parnell as a candidate, first in County Dublin, where he was unsuccessful in a by-election occasioned immediately after the 1874 general election by a ministerial appointment, and then in County Meath, where another by-election brought him victory, was a touch-and-go affair with many party pundits highly sceptical of his usefulness. After election speeches of an utterly unspectacular kind, badly delivered and scarcely coherent, it was not surprising that his stock remained low as he packed his bags for England.

Having a heart on the left over Home Rule and the tenants did not in itself signify much. It so happened that the very day Parnell took his seat as an M.P. Biggar made his first determined effort to 'Rub the English up' by parliamentary mischief. Biggar and his collaborator O'Connor Power had links with the Fenian movement. Their presence in parliament proved the inability of Fenianism totally to discredit constitutional agitation and soon these two men, led by Parnell, were to make hay of traditional Fenian policies so far as the vast majority of the Catholic masses were concerned. This change was not founded primarily on methods of protest, but on what the protests were about. Parnell's maiden speech was quite a tame affair; not so, however, what followed in the succeeding months. Though he had declared at Navan, on 7th October, 1875, that M.P.'s speeches were less important than votes,[1] his own later pronouncement that the 'Manchester Martyrs' had committed no murder[2] was worth a hundred votes in drawing attention to his extreme political position. Entering the United Kingdom parliament had deepened his hatred for the English. Like subsequent extreme nationalist, fascist and Communist parliamentarians he was in a liberal assembly to use it against itself, though, in his case, for a single reason—Ireland. There was no self-control in the air in 1876. Emotionalism was all. Very soon his innate political genius sized up the situation in parliament as well as in Ireland. He determined to lead his country to success and made himself the nodal point round which the new Nationalist party could centre. From the very first then he regarded the party he was

[1] R. Barry O'Brien, op. cit., p. 86.
[2] R. Barry O'Brien, op. cit., pp. 95–96.

to make as something unlike other parties and dependent upon him and him alone. This was a very subjective way of looking at the Irish question in 1876. Yet by 1877 he had been made President of the Home Rule Confederation of Great Britain and the process of working from the grassroots been set in motion. Nor was he now content with political radicalism alone. Whereas in the Meath campaign of 1875 he had only said; 'without fixity of tenure and fair rents the tenants would never be happy nor would the country be prosperous',[3] by the last months of 1877 he had become firmly convinced that 'the land question would never be settled on any other basis than that of giving to the Irish people the right and liberty of living on their own farms as owners'.[4] Doubtless the over-whelmingly rural nature of the Irish economy and the realization that only through enthusiastic backing from the peasantry could his ideal of Irish self-government stand a chance of being forced through by constitutional methods played a large part in making him shift his ground. At the same time, however, better knowledge of what was involved, an even clearer comprehension of the futility attaching to moderation and the dangerous downward plunge in the Irish agrarian economy pushed him in the same direction. The actual situation played into his hands. What was dictated by considerations of power the trend of events largely helped bring to fruition. The priority was self-government—as much of it as could be got. If a highly radical land policy improved the motive power of the Irish nationalist agitation,

[3] F. S. L. Lyons, 'The Economic Ideas of Parnell', in *Historical Studies*, II, ed. Roberts, p. 62.

[4] Ibid.

then a highly radical land policy there had to be. As over policy, so over methods. If direct action was impractical, then constitutionalism had to stay. The practical idealist in Parnell soon led him into the formulation of his fundamental ideological and methodological ideas. They were constantly adhered to.

Election to the Presidency of the Irish Nationalist organization in Britain marked for Parnell a triumph over Butt and the moderates in the ideological field and one over the pure milk Fenian Irish Republican Brotherhood men in that of method. That Parnell's behaviour in parliament differed profoundly from Butt's and that this difference had in no small degree been responsible for the former's success in winning back countless thousands of Irish nationalists to belief in parliamentary action and securing this valuable prestigious and potent position for himself must not, needless to say, be overlooked. Yet the policy differences between Parnell and Butt and the methodological differences between Parnell and the Fenian purists are the more crucial considerations to bear in mind. Being a non-Fenian of immense ability, the only man of truly first-class ability in the Home Rule parliamentary party, assured Parnell's unequalled value as a link between various elements of nationalist and nationalistic Irishmen. His extreme aims won him support within the inner circles of Fenianism well beyond the shores of the British isles. Prominent American Fenians, eminent in their organization the Clanna-Gael, began to court his favour. Despite the insistence of Devoy that Parnell entered into a definite compact with them termed the 'New Departure' this is doubtful. Besides being out of character for him to have tied his hands in this way, he himself denied having made it and the 'New Departure' which actually came into being was the result of something more than a pact between aspiring nationalists. In the early months of 1879 things had reached such a pitch in the Irish country-side that Davitt, one of the deserting Fenians, began setting up an organization amounting to what would now be regarded as a trade union for the protection of peasant interests. Devoy reasoned that if the Fenians helped the farmers, then the farmers would help the Fenians. Davitt went much further than this, and though converted to an unruly kind of constitutionalism, represented the extreme left in matters of social policy. Not for him any cold-blooded revolutionary's assessment of a power situation. The tenants' cause was for him an end in itself. Parnell stood midway between Devoy and Davitt. While arguing like Devoy about the rural masses, he was much more emotionally involved in their immediate material fate. While feeling for the tenantry, however, he was always wary lest the espousal of its cause should endanger his pet constitutional answer to the question as to how self-government was to be obtained. Admittedly, his statement at Tralee in November, 1878, that if it required an earthquake to solve the land question, then earthquake there would have to be,[5] committed him publicly to a 'root and branch' approach as well as solution. On the other hand, earthquakes can take place in parliament and he was always at pains to remark that justice would have to be done to the landlords. In the famous Westport speech of June 1879, when he openly declared support for Davitt's new type agitation,[6] this aspect

[5] R. Barry O'Brien, op. cit., p. 174.
[6] R. Barry O'Brien, op. cit., pp. 183–4.

of the issue received particular attention. His acceptance of the presidency of the Irish Land League in October of that year was another major step in the building up from the grass roots so essential to his plans for a united nationalist mass party. Although true that he accepted in order to moderate and control, his move related to methods not to policy content. Actions disturbing to the campaign at Westminster had to be ruled out, but the land for the 'People' was genuinely accepted by Parnell and it could fairly be said that he had very readily moved leftwards on the point. Davitt's socialist ideas for nationalizing Irish land were not generally taken up by the peasantry, so Parnell, in rejecting them, was not to the right of the masses of the agrarian mass movement. At the time of the 1880 general election, though, he was not converted to the principle of compulsion for land purchase, except in special circumstances. As president of the Land League he was nevertheless, temporarily obliged to abandon caution and publicly accept it. Not that this caused him any heartache. Tactical reasons alone had guided his initial position.

In the House of Commons the brunt of the new Irish effort was borne by Parnell and four others—Biggar, O'Donnell, O'Connor Power and Kirk. Their 'special satisfaction in preventing and thwarting the intentions of the Government'[7] earned them condemnation from British Conservatives and Liberals, backed by Butt and many of the moderate Home Rule politicians. By damaging the authority of the House of Commons Butt believed they were damaging 'the cause of representative government and of freedom all over the

[7] R. Barry O'Brien, op. cit., p. 132.

world'.[8] His warnings went unheeded. Indeed, Parnell actually liked antagonizing his political opponents because doing so created an added emotional barrier between them and him. He was afraid of the siren calls of Westminsterism and had seen the way it undermined the nationalistic convictions amongst the moderates. Not only then did obstruction bring home the realities of Irish discontent to Ministers and recharge the nationalist batteries amongst the Irish at home and abroad, but kept the 'ginger-group' fully gingered up. Fenian determination had impressed Parnell just as his usually excellent judgment and power of decision impressed the Fenians. The extreme wing knew that for this remarkable man parliamentarianism was a *pis aller*, that he had gone to Westminster to take it out of the British. The tone he adopted in parliamentary speeches was certainly more urbane than he used in public speeches whether on Irish or British platforms. But what did manner signify if the matter was essentially the same? His whole approach is well summed up by what he said at Manchester in July, 1877, to an audience of Irish resident in Lancashire: 'We will never gain anything from England, unless we tread upon her toes; we will never gain a single sixpennyworth from her by conciliation.'[9] In other words the British would only recognize power. While possibly true of governments, this was not true of a large slice of the electors behind them, but however important, perhaps crucial, his misjudgment on this point turned out to be, the very fact of making it at this time illustrates very well the lack of restraint and emotional self-indulgence so evident in the first phase of his career. The

[8] Moody, op. cit., p. 309.
[9] R. Barry O'Brien, op. cit., pp. 129–30.

methods were moderate, but the accompanying tone belied the moderation. His conception of the ideal future was a short period for mobilizing the Irish nation in a full-scale agitation led from parliament. Three or four years was the period mentioned from time to time. He made it all seem so easy. What T. M. Healy termed his 'commander-in-chief' quality impelled listeners into acceptance and what T. M. Healy termed his 'faculty of reducing a quarrel to the smallest dimensions' created a sense of unity and euphoria between those but lately at loggerheads.[10]

Hard fact told him that he must combine mastery over the restless rural masses with the best possible relations with the Catholic Church. In this first phase mastery over that body was unthinkable. Not until lay Catholicism and a large proportion of the lower clergy had enthusiastically endorsed his leadership did the hierarchy and its immediate entourage turn a friendly eye upon him. Even the nationalist Archbishop MacHale condemned the Westport meeting, and though this was probably because the rackrenting landlord under attack was one of his priests, no such special considerations weighed with Archbishop MCabe, whose disapprobation of such activities was deepseated and vociferous. The Land League scandalized almost the whole hierarchy. Its whole weight in by-elections was thrown behind the forces of moderation— Buttite or Whig. Parnell was not a man to avoid a battle that had to be fought. Events obliged him to move fast and the prospects were good. Also, he knew his men and was not afraid. The moderates had to be hammered. The masses wanted them hammered. Even amongst the limited electorate

[10] R. Barry O'Brien, op. cit., p. 103.

the desire to hammer them was widespread. Collision with local bishops was therefore inevitable, if everyone stuck to their guns. One big advantage lay with Parnell from the beginning. Many lower clergy were at least sympathetic to Fenianism and found the aims of Parnell in parliament and the Land League in Ireland highly congenial. The methods in vogue appealed to rather than disgusted them. The hierarchy could not command uniform political obedience. While the League was in embryo a by-election took place at Ennis. Despite vigorous clerical support the Whig candidate was defeated. Parnell's comment was typical: 'If Ennis had been lost I would have retired from public life, for it would have satisfied me that the priests were supreme in Irish politics'.[11] The key word is 'supreme'. He did not mean to imply that Catholic priests should have no place in Irish political life, but the one he envisaged for them was as subordinates in his party. They in turn would have to play at going to Canossa. But the process was only just begun when the general election of 1880 arrived. Many priests were involved with the Land League, yet neutrality was the best Parnell got out of the bishops. Where moderate fought Parnellite episcopal blessings flowed fast and furious to the former. Where a Parnellite was

[11] R. Barry O'Brien, op. cit., p. 191. A good illustration of the way Parnell managed his relations with the Catholic Church is his behaviour over the Bradlaugh case. Although really on Bradlaugh's side at the outset, for a number of political and social reasons, he swung round to the position favoured by the bulk of his party and the Catholic Church once it appeared politic to do so. For this see Walter L. Arnstein, 'Parnell and the Bradlaugh case', *Irish Historical Studies*, 1963; and the same author's book, *The Bradlaugh Case: A Study in Late Victorian Opinion and Politics*, 1965.

the sole 'Irish' aspirant there was often a somewhat unbenevolent neutrality. The struggle to show who was the 'Master' was still being fought out. The left of Irish nationalism was in Parnell's bag. Its support was vital, for the pace-making element in Irish politics thereby passed to him. A little before the general election Irish America had endorsed the 'New Departure' to the tune of 200,000 dollars, subscribed during his 11,000 mile tour of the United States. The centre was moving towards the left as the plight of the tenant farmers severely worsened and the revolutionary left was drifting rightwards because of Parnell. The right was extremely vulnerable electorally, despite the narrow franchise, but the new nationalism trod warily in the general election. It fought where victory was already virtually assured. Out of Ireland's 103 M.P.'s only 24 would appear to have been full-blooded Parnellite Home Rulers as the election ended. There were, however, 21 moderate Home Rulers and 14 of an indeterminate allegiance. Parnell was elected Sessional Chairman of the Irish Home Rule party in May, 1880 and its moderate wing soon disintegrated. Two of its members went over to Parnell along with most of the hitherto uncommitted. In January, 1881, twelve moderates, including Shaw, Butt's nominal successor as Sessional chairman and Parnell's unsuccessful rival for the post, seceded from the party to become virtual supporters of the Liberals. In the words of C. C. O'Brien: 'After May 1880 the Parnellite group tends to become for most practical purposes, the home rule party'.[12] Nothing succeeds like success. As Parnell championed the idea of a Catholic university, wanted all the Irishmen he

[12] C. C. O'Brien, op. cit., p. 26.

could get behind his banner and already enjoyed the active help of many humble priests, the stage was set for a tactful adjustment of policy by the hierarchy.

The new Nationalist party pivoted round its leader. He had achieved success without subterfuge or the exercise of sustained self-control. His delicate nerves had been soothed by the ready response great qualities of leadership had found in so many quarters. Both Fenian and Ribbonist type traditions had found an emotional outlet in the new cause. Sheer brilliance had established his hegemony such as it was, sheer brilliance was to maintain and extend it. The need for maintenance was inherent in the situation. Some Fenianism had declined to be swallowed up. During the election campaign at Enniscorthy extremists attacked the Home Rule platform with the cry that they would show Parnell that the blood of Vinegar Hill was still 'green'. This problem was to remain with him during the next two phases of his career and to combat it what better instrument was there than the priesthood? Moves had to be made to show men like Archbishop Croke that they could safely put their shirts on the new leader without condoning violence. Then a counterweight would exist in the party to help control the left. For the English Parnell thought bullying the only treatment. Even where sympathy for the Irish people was strongest—on the Liberal left—pressure was quite ruthlessly applied. A Home Rule pledge was made the price of the Irish vote. The system had been used by Butt. Now, while the idea remained the same, there was a new iron in the Irish attitude. Parnell's emotional self-indulgence had spread out into the constituencies. So adroit in charming Irish birds off countless trees, his distaste for his opponents led him into neglecting the state of their feelings. He was to pay a heavy price for his pains. Nevertheless, this was way ahead and in 1880 everything was going well. It is vital to see that the main lines of policy are clear. Only ruin was to change them in 1890. The change from the Conservative inactivity of 1874–80 to the Liberal 'stop-go' policy of 1880–85 drew nothing fundamentally new from our great man's political laboratory.

4 Consolidation, Opportunity and Advance

While true that the tactics of the years 1880–85 were highly complicated, the strategy had a stark simplicity. Now Parnell had the party leadership in his hands the aim was to create a highly disciplined force in parliament with a firm grip over all other nationalist activity. Under the conditions obtaining at the outset an excess of parliamentary individualists presented something of a complication. All these would-be pundits had to be swamped by reliable lobby fodder. Then, too, individual branches or members of the Land League were liable to run amok periodically and endanger the 'Grand Design' for attaining self-government by precipitate actions embarrassing to the parliamentary party. To say that what happened was all part of a carefully formulated plan would be nonsense. To say that Parnell worked hard to exploit the openings offered to him and succeeded overall in creating a system of safeguards against unsubtle and penurious enthusiasts would not. For the poor farmer or labourer patience was difficult to muster. Hardship was actually at their doors. Parnell knew this and endeavoured to use the maximum amount of agitation in and out of parliament consistent with adherence to the notion of securing relief through constitutional means. The Whig-dominated Gladstone government began by trying to ignore Irish problems. Carefully calculated tactics prodded them into introducing a Compensation for Disturbance Bill. The 'New Departure' seemed to be working well. When the House of Lords rejected the Bill widespread agitation broke out in Ireland. Of the 2,590 agrarian crimes committed during 1880, more than half took place in the last three months of the year (i.e. after the Bill's rejection). Sparks from the grassroots warned of a possible flare up and Parnell saw it was necessary to impress the government with the feeling and danger in the situation. Moreover, to carry more weight in the House of Commons a convincing demonstration that his party was heartily backed in its homeland was no bad thing. Speaking at Ennis in September the leader pulled no punches and openly advocated what became known as boycotting; '. . . he warned his hearers that the land bill of the next session would be the measure of their determination not to pay unjust rents and not to take farms from which others had been evicted'.[1] Now, of course, the Liberal government had it in its power to smash the agitation, but its ethos would not allow blank negation in face of public discontent. The policy of 'Kicks and Kindness' was therefore applied. Parnell and other prominent Nationalists were arrested and unsuccessfully tried. Coercion was passed amidst scenes of intense bitterness in the House of Commons. But, this was crucial, a generous Land Act was also passed giving the long desired 'Three F's'. The 'New Departure'

[1] R. Barry O'Brien, op. cit., pp. 236–7.

had won three victories—its leader enjoyed a much-enhanced prestige and Clan-na-Gael whisperings came to naught, the government had failed to get him convicted of anything, and a great concession had been prised out of the United Kingdom parliament. There had been scant emotional self-restraint exercised by Parnell in or out of the House of Commons. Seldom can constitutional politics have been so explosive. If this is what C. C. O'Brien means by a personal inclination pulling to the right, then his explanation is inadequate. As Emmet Larkin is at pains to make clear, Irish politics have a spectrum ranging from revolution to the extreme right.[2] Surely, given Parnell's belief that power alone impressed the British, there is no real ground for supposing that such a passionate man should have been play acting at Ennis? What C. C. O'Brien should have clarified is the existence of different types of extremism. To talk of Parnell wanting to move rightwards can be profoundly misleading in a tactical, let alone a strategic context. Having the high command in his hands and being able to decide when hell was to be let loose was quite a different thing from wanting a policy of perpetual talking. No one knew better than Parnell the need to talk from strength. We have here the old danger of confusing means with ends plus a semantic muddle about the precise meaning of 'rightwards'. Truly there were two kinds of extremism current in Irish politics. That outside the 'New Departure' (attractive to many within it) and that championed by Parnell. The latter kind was based on parliamentary action with controlled outbursts at the grassroots acting as a sup-

---

[2] Emmet Larkin, 'The Roman Catholic Hierarchy and the Fall of Parnell', *Victorian Studies*, 1961, p. 335.

plement. Merely to stress Parnell's quest for a parliamentary solution ignores his scorn for Butt, his great hurry, and what actually happened. Admittedly, he may have been concerned lest his control should be lost, yet can there really be any doubt that acting with the Land League as he did merely involved his head according with his heart. Nor was he alone. Moderate forces like the 'Freeman's Journal' showed a burning indignation at this time. In short, the storms of 1880–81 generally fitted in well with both the mood and desires of the new Irish Nationalist parliamentary party. Allies too stood firm. Few priests turned squeamish under the impact of conflict.

During the Coercion Bill debates no fewer than 36 Nationalist M.P.'s had been suspended—almost the whole of the now much-extended Parnellite party. Occasionally, Parnell had pleased extremist hotheads by threatening withdrawal from Westminster and some have seen in his failure to do so at this particular juncture proof of inherent moderation. The same has been said about his refusal to reject the 1881 Land Act out of hand. Over the first it is difficult to understand just why the expulsion alone should have guided any shrewd leader. Legislation was the sole practical way to self-government, the new party had only just found its feet and Irish Nationalism had plenty of room for expanding its parliamentary representation at the next general election, whether or not the franchise had been widened. Why then leave parliament when things were at half cock? Why leave parliament when national unity back in Ireland was still an unfinished edifice? There was never any serious reason for supposing Parnell would ever contemplate abandoning attendance at Westminster unless

constitutionalism failed. So far as he could judge at that point
the government would grant him the land reform he wanted
just as it had taken up compensation for disturbance. He was
right. Over the second it would have been looking a valuable
gift horse in the mouth to reject the Land Act. Testing it out
meant revealing its inadequacies and preparing the ground for
further reforms. Outright acceptance was, nonetheless, another matter and such was the furore he helped foment
following the implementation of the Act that the government
decided to cast him into Kilmainham gaol. Both Professor
Lyons and C. C. O'Brien have seen in the arrangement leading to his release a decisive strengthening of constitutional
politics.[3] Davitt regarded it as a vital change in the wrong
direction.[4] In fact, what shift there was affected tactics alone.
The strategy remained essentially the same. At Galway, in
October 1880, Parnell had avowed he 'would not have taken
off his coat' over the land war 'if he had not thought it would
lead to the independence of Ireland'.[5] That is, he considered
that at that time the agitation helped rather than hindered his
pet design. There was no reason to think differently after
the Land Act was passed, for it left leaseholders out in the cold
and the arrears question unsolved. Arrest and incarceration
strengthened this hold over the masses and played into the
hands of 'Captain Moonlight'. The grassroots tended to glow

[3] Lyons, *The Fall of Parnell*, p. 13; *Parnell*, p. 12. C. C. O'Brien,
op. cit., p. 78.

[4] M. Davitt, *The Fall of Feudalism*, p. 349. The remark of Sir
Edward, later Lord Carson, that only a fool would fight when he could
avoid doing so was a lesson Parnell had learned at an early stage of his
political career.

[5] R. Barry O'Brien, op. cit., pp. 239–40.

a little too brightly for Gladstone's liking and Parnell acquired at last something of the value in the eyes of the government necessary for pushing the Home Rule cause ahead. His profound pessimism about the state of the movement, seemingly confirmed by the failure of the 'No Rent' manifesto, was quite misplaced. Just as he had been on the verge of despair his tactics paid off and the handsome bonus—the Kilmainham 'Treaty'—bulging in his political pockets had got there without any sacrifice of Nationalist strategy. He was not asked to accept the Land Act as it stood, but only after amendment to cover those matters about which he had agitated immediately prior to imprisonment—undeniably a considerable score for 'New Departure' politics. Coercion, which as Davitt foresaw, had smashed the Land League and threatened the new nationalism with severe setbacks, was to be dropped —another clear success. The price demanded by the government was low. All Parnell had to do was 'use his influence against outrage and intimidation in Ireland'—things already severely crushed by coercion—and 'co-operate cordially for the future with the liberal party in forwarding liberal principles and measures of general reform' [6]—something which, if interpreted freely, he had been doing since entering parliament, and which would enable him to accumulate more capital in the Liberal bank to draw on for the winning of Irish self-government. The mixture of defiant parliamentary agitation backed by severe yet unrevolutionary agitation in Ireland had been a happy one. That it was not used again in exactly the same way immediately, or for that matter later on, was not due to any cooling of the leader's determination or basic nationalist con-

[6] C. C. O'Brien, op. cit., p. 77.

victions. Different situations call for changes in tactics. Quiet approaches employed from his release in May 1882 indicated not the end of uncertainty as to whether or not to be a constitutionalist—he had always been that—but the end of the time when the old mixture could effectively be applied. In Ireland he used his increased authority to squeeze out the Ladies' Land League, improvised to replace the suppressed Land League, and launch the Irish National League, centrally controlled by the parliamentary party. To keep the leftist enthusiasts happy the ten month old 'United Ireland' (edited by W. O'Brien) presented constitutional politics as just another form of outrage and intimidation. Dillon and W. O'Brien loyally accepted the plan, even the retreat in the National League programme from full-scale application of compulsion in Land Purchase, and the terrible Phoenix Park murders perpetrated by the non-Parnellite left triggered off a series of reactions facilitating still further a move away from old methods. Once again circumstances helped Parnell. His left elements were put in a weak position just at the time when he wanted them kept quiet. Because most of its adherents did not understand the difference between an extreme end and an extreme means a psychological campaign for soothing them was required. Again good fortune came to the rescue in the form of W. O'Brien and 'United Ireland'.

While the Phoenix Park murders watered down the Kilmainham arrangement as regards its actual terms, its spirit survived them virtually intact. British public opinion demanded and got more coercion, but its effect was to help Parnell. The resistance offered to it by the parliamentary Nationalist party lacked the fervour of the year before. Shock and horror had been the general Irish response to news of the

murders. The cult of violence had sunk low in public esti-
mation. After all, morality apart, what good was it compared
with the spit and polish of the Parnellite movement? For
many there was too much polish and too little spit. Men like
Davitt did not like the diplomatic element in politics. For
them moving out of the last stretch of desert into the first few
miles of the 'Promised Land' was a painful experience. Lacking Parnell's genius and subtlety they mistook appearance for
reality. Their emotionalism took an unintelligent form. Not so
Parnell's. His offer to Gladstone to withdraw from public life
because of the Phoenix Park affair was made at a moment
when his whole work appeared to lay in ruins. It betokened
an over-excited not a foolish response to the situation. Gladstone's advice to remain and the situation in Ireland soon
calmed him down. Both sides of the operation—parliamentary
and domestic—appeared to be going well. The government
quickly tackled the arrears question and seemed likely to
undertake franchise reform. Coercion and delay over the
leaseholders would be a small price to pay for the means of
demonstrating the vast mass support for the new Nationalist
party. To argue that Parnell's contacts with the government
began before Kilmainham and that therefore he favoured
moderation before it was necessary is to miss the point.
Naturally, he wanted to achieve his ends with the minimum of
trouble. All political avenues had to be explored and if one to
the government opened up so much the better. The crucial
fact was that when nothing resulted he still continued agitation. After Kilmainham things changed. Not only was the
government responsive and eager to keep Parnell in public life, but agitation had become unwise and superfluous.

Franchise reform was always in Parnell's mind. He had long appreciated the significance of elections and electioneering. It did not take imprisonment to concentrate his mind. Loose support was therefore given to government on general policy to keep the Liberal party sweet on franchise reform. That this relationship held good is proved by one fact above all. The Conservatives had to bribe Parnell to give it up. On the domestic front the party extended and consolidated its power and influence. Papal letters fell on virtually deaf ears and the drift of priests and pious laymen into the Parnellite camp quickened remarkably. In 1884 the hierarchy actually sought the aid of the parliamentary party on educational matters. They had no alternative unless they risked neglecting their duties. Electorally things went extremely well. The contests were generally mopping up operations run by the priests and the National League. Candidates tended to be produced by a committee in Dublin and rubber-stamped by conventions of reliable supporters. This was a far cry from Land League days. Nevertheless, machinery can be overstressed. Without a change in mood and a shift in the centre of gravity in the party, organization could have achieved little. The Church had had to condemn a 'No Rent' policy; it could warm to parliamentary diplomacy spliced with organization. The 'solid classes' shied away from violence but warmed to discussion. The violent men had either to break out and fail, or wait and see. Parnell's prestige and surrounding circumstances were such as to make them opt for the less heroic alternative.

During 1883 no less than £40,000 were collected from the Irish masses for Parnell. Characteristically, he accepted the present without a word of thanks. No offence was taken, even by priests whose participation in the scheme had had ultimately to be clandestine because of condemnation by the Holy Office. Equally characteristically he was quick to see the firm hold he had come to have over the Irish nationalist scene generally. America's Irish too had formed a National League controlled by Clan-na-Gael. Its policy reflected strongly his appeal for prudence and restraint. At Drogheda in April 1884 he made a bold move towards clarifying still further the Nationalist party's policy on the land.[7] Davitt's nostra about nationalization were unceremoniously cast aside. Landlords would have to be compensated. Land ownership was not in itself inherently evil and the two aims to be pursued were lower rents and Land Purchase. The National League policy of compensation was reaffirmed. 'You must either fight for the land or pay for it,'[8] he declared, knowing full well only one method was open to his hearers. Four months later the famous party pledge for Nationalist candidates was introduced. It committed aspirants to a promise of sitting, acting and voting with the Irish Nationalist party in the House of Commons and of resigning if that party deemed their conduct unsatisfactory. Everyone was obliged to accept it. Then came the long awaited franchise extension. The Irish electorate was more than trebled. And, what is more, the change was crucial for borough as well as county constituencies. Parnell was on top of the party and the party was on top of the Catholic masses. Leading British Radicals like Chamberlain and Dilke favoured

---

[7] R. Barry O'Brien, *The Life of Charles Stewart Parnell*, Vol. II, pp. 34–36. Lyons, 'The Economic Ideas of Parnell', in *Historical Studies*, II, ed. Roberts, p. 69.

[8] Ibid.

the granting of extensive local government to Ireland, and, although the Liberal Cabinet turned down their plan, Gladstone, Cardinal Manning, and the Irish hierarchy were known to favour it.[9] It was at this point that Parnell demonstrated the ruthless nature of his strategy and his reliance on power for dealing with the British. The Radical leaders proposed visiting Ireland in pursuit of their new ideas. This posed a possible threat to the newly extended Parnellite edifice, for the hierarchy might accept as a final settlement what Parnell himself regarded as an interim dividend. The Radicals intended it to be the former and thought the Irish leader did too, but he had never attempted to mislead them. Both sides had their go-between, Captain O'Shea, to thank for the confusion. Fortune once more rescued Parnell from an awkward situation. The Conservatives began to flirt with him. His aim of getting hold of the British political leadership had been carried one stage further. Liberalism had reached an especially troublesome phase and nowhere was this more apparent than in Irish policy. With typical humorous exaggeration Harcourt suggested the muddle be cleared up with a programme of: 'No Home Rule, no coercion, no remedial legislation, no Ireland at all'. Britain would have leapt at such a scheme had circum-

[9] Lyons, *Parnell*, p. 15, claims Chamberlain was 'too far in advance of his party' in advocating the 'central board', or 'National Councils' scheme. It would be truer to say the Cabinet was way behind large sections of the party on this issue. Glorified local government was not Home Rule and every commoner member of the Cabinet, except Hartington, favoured Chamberlain's plan. All the peers, except Granville, were against it. The majority was certainly less in touch with preponderant feeling in the party on this point—and many others for that matter—than the Chamberlain-led minority, which included Gladstone.

stances not ruled it out. Those circumstances could be summed up largely in the word 'Parnell'. To that word the Conservatives now paid a self-interested attention. Randolph Churchill's contacts with the Irish leader overflowed with innuendoes. What was clear, however, was that if the Nationalists would help the Conservatives to push Gladstone's tottering second Ministry from office and support a Conservative replacement against the Liberals, an instalment of Land Purchase would be given, coercion would not be renewed and certain judicial proceedings would be looked into. June 1885 saw the end of the second Ministry. Parnell had demonstrated he was not part of the United Kingdom 'Left', whatever fond hopes had been cherished on that score. His breach of the Kilmainham agreement had a justification, for coercion had again been in force and the leaseholders still awaited relief under the second Land Act. Whether full Liberal implementation of Kilmainham would have had an effect on the situation no one can say, but Parnell had an especially powerful motive for switching towards the Conservatives quite unconnected with the past. He aimed to hold the balance in the House of Commons between the two United Kingdom parties and knew the Conservatives controlled the House of Lords.[10] So sure in his

[10] In his pamphlet on *Parnell* Lyons argues that Parnell favoured dealing with the Conservatives, not only because they controlled the House of Lords, but because 'they were likely to be much more tender towards the landlords—the backbone of Irish Unionism'. If by this is meant that soft treatment of the landlords would make a Home Rule settlement easier to obtain, the facts belie the claim. One, if not the major reason why Gladstone failed to get his first Home Rule Bill through the House of Commons was the furore raised by the generous terms envisaged in a concomitant Land Bill. Even its withdrawal failed to undo the mischief. Nor would any amount of generosity soften up

touch of Irish affairs, he showed himself crude and insensitive on some points in judging British matters. Yet he was correct in his estimate of what would happen if the Irish Nationalist voters in Britain were instructed to vote against all but a handful of Liberals.[11] Before that happened an interview with the new Viceroy, held in secret, had revealed him as favouring some form of Home Rule. Whilst Lord Caernarvon had made a point of saying he spoke only for himself, Parnell could hardly be blamed for attaching some importance to what he learned. Lord Salisbury, the new Prime Minister delivered a masterpiece of *suppressio veri suggestio falsi* at Newport some little time later and Nationalist circles nearly burst with expectation. When Gladstone appealed to the electorate for the chance to settle the Irish question independently of Parnell, the need to cast the Irish vote for Conservative candidates was more than clear. The upshot of the 1885 general election was that Parnell did hold the fate of United Kingdom governments in his hand. 86 fully pledged and excited Irish Nationalists held the balance in the House of Commons. In mid-December came the indiscretion known as the 'Hawarden Kite'. Gladstone, the man for whom Parnell regarded himself as no match, was apparently a convert to the principle of Home Rule. Denials were useless, for everyone realized a cat had been let out of the G.O.M.'s famous bag.

Phase two had ended. For the first time in history the Irish Catholic masses were thoroughly represented in the House of

landlord opinion. Although the series of Land Purchase Acts weakened the power of Unionism outside the 'Six Counties', it did not affect its pretensions one tittle.

[11] See Appendix.

Commons. By trusting Parnell they had created the motive force to make the pace in United Kingdom politics. Many have seen a rightward trend in the advent of the supremacy of the parliamentary party. Why is far from clear. Parnell had no real parliamentary party before 1880. In the first year or two of *de jure* leadership he had to establish a parliamentary machine. But as it always had been his intention to build up power in parliament and the 'New Departure' had had the same thing as its *raison d'être*, the whole process here explained was simply a fulfilment of a wish felt by those elements of the Irish left not irrevocably wedded to strong arm methods. Maybe the decline of opportunities to revert to old ways could be interpreted as a rightist trend. But, as subsequent history was to show, renewal of rural distress could recreate these without straining unduly the party machine as it stood in completed form. Policy continued radical. Parnell bargained hard for the maximum political, social and economic concessions he could get. Constitutional politics had brought him allies who would have been satisfied with far less. Could there be any real doubt, though, that they were with him because they could not be against? The hierarchy had not pronounced officially for Home Rule by December 1885, but would their having pronounced against it and for the Chamberlain scheme have had much effect on the 1885 election results? Most probably not, with Parnell as leader of the left and the past record of priests supporting him pointing to the very real limitations suffered from by the episcopacy in politics. Alliance for tactical reasons with those believing in cautious tactics and strategy should not necessarily be thought to drag an organization rightwards. What counts is who holds the initiative and basic power. In this instance it was Parnell and his lieutenants. Expansion of party numbers had tightened rather than decreased their control over Nationalist M.P.'s. The humbler social origins of many among the newer recruits did not lead to moves for a return to agitation unsynchronized with parliamentary plans.

Parnell himself had displayed the same qualities as before. Deep emotion drove him on in his great power building operation. Of basic self-restraint there was little. The game went his way with remarkably minimized risk. His ability saved him untold strain. Brilliance brought him success and commonsense told him when to rest. Illicit love could have been a terrible burden. As things turned out at this stage it was exactly the contrary. When the fight had burnt him out Mrs. O'Shea offered repose and means of recovery. Love or no love his sense of economy would probably have caused him to drop out of day to day affairs for long periods. For such a singled-minded person times when his ideas could not be directly furthered were not times to wear himself out attending to inconsequentialities. A keen sense of priorities had dictated adherence to parliament. On occasion it dictated absence from it. Phase three was to see this repeated. The practice had results some of which were potentially dangerous for Parnell. It gave the party openings for an existence independent of him that would not otherwise have arisen. Building up belief in constitutional action had largely succeeded and propaganda had effectively linked the party with the craving for land in the minds of the masses. That the party commanded respect as such and the tendencies of its members to be constitutionalists in precept as well as in deed could in certain conditions prove dangerous to its leader's personal ascendancy. Great though that was, the 'personal spell' theory often put forward to explain it has been vastly overplayed. The protection issue alone provides an important instance of how much. Whereas the horizons of most Irish Nationalists were bounded by the wish for self-government and agrarian reform, Parnell's stretched further into the realms of future possibilities. That he took the industrialization of his country seriously aligns him with countless modern nationalist extremists. The notion involved the desire for autarchy, or something approaching it. At the interview with Lord Caernarvon the matter had been raised *unter vielen Augen.* In several speeches delivered at Nationalist gatherings about the same time—mid 1885—Parnell made much of his dreams. His efforts fell flat.[12] For a breakthrough great effort was required. Yet preoccupation with the immediate and the consequent absence from the fray meant it was not forthcoming. Perhaps this was just as well for the Home Rule cause, but it showed there were very real limits to the 'Uncrowned King's' authority. Phase three was in one respect a paradox. It showed how the near omnipotent often had to tolerate near insubordination.

[12] See Lyons, 'The Economic Ideas of Parnell' in *Historical Studies,* II, ed. Roberts, pp. 70–71.

5   Great Expectations

Within a month of the 'Hawarden Kite' a Liberal-Nationalist alliance was well on the way. However much Gladstone had come to favour the principle of Irish self-government, force of circumstances certainly speeded up his quest to have it put into practice. When the Conservative effort to baffle and crush the Liberal party by using Nationalist aid came to naught, the Salisbury Cabinet disowned the Caernarvon view and prepared to fall back on a fresh dose of coercion. The 1885 election had not ended the Conservatives' demotion to the smaller British party and Salisbury wished to court parliamentary defeat on an issue best calculated to increase support. Ireland was as good a bet as any. Gladstone's acuteness stalled him. The G.O.M. contrived to have the government thrown out with Parnell's aid while avoiding a specific vote on the Irish Home Rule issue. Parnell seemed to have won all round and Gladstone's aid indicated shrewdness and skill would increasingly be at the Nationalists' disposal. Why then was Home Rule not accepted by the House of Commons? What went wrong? The answer is to be found in the link up between the powerful objections of wealthy interests in the United Kingdom and the powerful anti-Catholic and anti-Hibernian feelings among sections of what might be termed the floating vote of the British electorate. Parnell had made the Nationalist parliamentary party from the grassroots, yet pursued his campaign against the English at the leadership level. At that level he had succeeded, but Gladstone's authority, like his own, was not boundless. Important sections of the parliamentary Liberal party revolted, and, substantial though some popular pressure in favour of Gladstone was, found support in circles not usually Conservative for what they had done. Even before the Home Rule Bill was defeated on its second reading in June, 1886, Parnell had lost the balance in terms of numbers in the House of Commons. The Conservative decision to stand or fall by the Union had lost him it in terms of parties even earlier. But had he won the hearts of the English with that allegedly irresistible charm and simplicity, had he really been so universally cool and calculating in the way that is often claimed to have been an essential part of him, then a Commons defeat would not have been all that much of a setback. The subsequent general election would have given Gladstone a sizeable majority, in which case the House of Lords might well have caved in without creating a major constitutional crisis. Ulster would then have been left high and dry. Public opinion would have been an important support for getting his way. Had the G.O.M. actually won a majority so large as to make him independent of Parnell, this would, of course, have meant a reduction in Nationalist bargaining strength, but not any change in the fundamental position. At that stage the

87

'Union of Hearts' would have been too healthy for that. Instead, he had chosen to wage a very restricted kind of 'cold war' with an almost entirely negative psychological side. For this error he paid a heavy price. The Conservative and Liberal Unionist parties won the election following the defeat of the Home Rule Bill. The probable cost of Land Purchase to the imperial exchequer had been a factor in bringing on both the parliamentary and the electoral setbacks. For the moment it seemed that social as well as political reform was blocked. Whatever the truth was, phase three brought him the long haul he had always dreaded so much. It involved close relationships with the Liberals at a social as well as a business level. To get British opinion on his side and make up for the past he was obliged to do the very thing he had resisted for so long—expose the Irish Nationalists to the full impact of another seductive force besides himself. That force was British left wing democracy. In the past he had forbidden T. M. Healy to dine with Chamberlain. Because Chamberlain had become a leading Liberal Unionist that contingency was unlikely to recur, but any Nationalist M.P. could now keep the company of Labouchère and Morley with impunity. The party's freedom of manoeuvre became severely restricted from the time when the contents of the Home Rule Bill had been agreed upon and, what is more, Parnell had been obliged to abandon all hopes of protection. During the great debate he publicly acknowledged his retraction on that point. With seven years of Conservative government in prospect all this was aggravated by the likelihood of unrest on the home front. Agrarian conditions were again undergoing another period of chronic deterioration. Not that everything looked

black. Early in the year the Catholic hierarchy had at last
officially espoused the Home Rule cause. About the same time
Parnell had been able to demonstrate his immense power by
foisting none other than the gallant Captain O'Shea upon the
electors of Galway City as their M.P. A minor rebellion led
by Biggar and T. M. Healy never got going, despite direct
references to the leader's illicit relations with the Captain's
wife. Unpledged and Whiggish, O'Shea later enjoyed the
distinction of being the sole Nationalist M.P. to vote against
the Home Rule Bill. American money had again flowed freely
in the months of expectation. In August 1886 Davitt and W.
O'Brien crossed the Atlantic and secured a thumping vote of
confidence for the new concept of a 'Union of Hearts'. Acts
of Irish-American terrorism ceased forthwith. Something else
was also of prime importance. Parnell had never pledged himself not to pursue independence.

He tackled the 1886 post-election situation much as he had
that of 1880, introducing into parliament a measure of agrarian
relief. Evictions were to be stayed. Failure, however, had
very different consequences this time. In 1880 he had himself led the subsequent agitation in Ireland, besides defying
parliament. Now he stuck to parliament alone and what was
known as the 'Plan of Campaign' was run by Dillon and
W. O'Brien more or less against his wishes. His objections
were tactical. There was no question of his having gone 'soft'
on the landlords. But the whole affair illustrates very well the
limitations of his authority when something fundamental
divided him from the bulk of his following. When the land
issue was quiescent moderation was not seriously challenged.
Having Home Rule in the hollow of his hand meant Galway

City was eventually prepared to swallow the unpledged O'Shea. Now things were different. As before, shrewdness and circumstances came to his rescue. Careful handling of his lieutenants and a cunning use of Liberal pressure secured a series of restrictions on the agitation. He thereby kept the Liberals from becoming too unhappy without offending many of the Irish. On the other hand such trouble as there was remained a threat to law and order. Spring 1887 saw the introduction of a Coercion Bill and in July the National League was 'proclaimed'. Nationalist unity was again augmented, the more so as Parnell never attempted to deter his M.P.'s from agitating and getting themselves arrested! No fewer than 24 had been to prison by Spring 1889. As before the government made concessions. Its 1887 Land Act not only lessened the possibility of eviction, but at last brought leaseholders the benefits of the 1881 Act. Even before it was passed, though, actual agitation or threat of it had substantially decreased the eviction rate. And the whole situation was given a new twist when the hierarchy declined to condemn the 'Plan of Campaign'.

Under the Conservatives as under the Liberals Parnell accepted most government concessions quite readily. His opposition to the 1890 Land Bill was due entirely to exceptional Liberal pressure and is the sole departure from the general rule. When necessary he swept any suspicion of inactivity aside and acted with resolution. In 1889 he promptly answered the formation of an Irish landlords syndicate with a Tenants' Defence League and did not stand in the way of the 'New Tipperary' scheme, under which a new series of shops was provided by the 'Plan' campaigners to replace boycotted ones. Financial problems abounded and the prominence of Dillon and W. O'Brien built up their importance, yet his command was assured and he fast secured a wealth of sympathy from the Gladstonian electorate, largely through the introduction of coercion. The government took the position less calmly. Phase three saw several determined bids to smash Irish nationalism by means of personal vilification and ecclesiastical condemnation. Both boomeranged badly. Just as the 1887 Coercion Bill was before the House of Commons the 'Times' newspaper published letters appearing to implicate Parnell in the Phoenix Park murders. At a subsequent Special Commission, amounting to an indirect means of having an unofficial state trial of Parnell and his party, these letters were exposed as forgeries and the British left fell over backwards to make up in friendship for the right wing enmity revealed by the slur. December 1889 brought Parnell to the height of distinction—he was invited by Gladstone to Hawarden Castle. When the Papal authorities pronounced against the 'Plan of Campaign' and boycotting in April 1888 their anathemas fell completely flat. The hierarchy did little or nothing and most of the Nationalist laity ignored them. The following month Parnell demonstrated his inherent power as a leader by publicly revealing his lack of enthusiasm for the 'Plan of Campaign' and ignoring the Pope altogether. The occasion was a Liberal dinner at the 'Eighty Club', where Gladstone also spoke. Next day a Home Rule address signed by no fewer than 3,730 nonconformist ministers declared the Conservatives to be the true authors of the 'Plan'. The mood of that dinner had by the close of 1890 become the mood of the vast majority of Liberals and Irish Nationalists. The government had failed to 'Kill

Home Rule by Kindness' or unkindness. By-elections in Britain itself were, for a variety of reasons, going against Unionism throughout almost the whole of this third phase. Things looked favourable for the 'Union of Hearts'. Five years before most Nationalists had been eager for separation from Britain in their heart of hearts. Greater power, and surprise at having got it, had mellowed them. Many became believers in what had initially been a working compromise. Jam tomorrow seemed infinitely preferable to ambrosia next week. Suddenly everything was in disarray, and the cause—the man who had brought them so far. Phase four had begun.

6 *Disgrace, Decline and Death*

What Emmet Larkin terms 'Parnell's uncanny and effective judgment in the moment of crisis, a subtle touch for the levers of power, and the utter unscrupulousness of a man convinced of his "mission" '[1] were never better displayed at a tactical level than in the last months of his life. Strategy was quite a different kettle of fish. However he himself viewed things it was profoundly changed. The change was for the worse, for he treated the continuance of his leadership as an end in itself and inevitably pushed Home Rule into the position of the second priority. What brought all this about was, of course, the successful outcome of a divorce suit filed by Captain O'Shea. At first disaster had been slow in developing. The only consequences when the suit was initially filed in December 1889 were rapturous votes of confidence from all Nationalist quarters. Even after O'Shea got his way and

[1] Emmet Larkin, 'Mounting the Counter-Attack: The Roman Catholic Hierarchy and the Destruction of Parnellism', *Review of Politics*, 1963, p. 159.

Parnell had been adjudicated an adulterer, his own assurances, the great faith in him, recent British attempts to blemish his character and a vigorous nationalism all militated strongly in his favour. The Catholic hierarchy was loth to intervene against him on moral grounds when the masses whose political views they favoured were still so enthusiastically loyal to his leadership. Ireland's general reaction to what had happened was well typified by his re-election to the Nationalist party chairmanship eight days after the fateful court decision. Unhappily, the moral indignation of British Nonconformity was all too soon to shatter this mood of 'follow the leader'. Davitt's lone voice of protest became drowned by a concurring chorus of bitter disapproval. When the parliamentary party had given a clear sign of having a majority for abandoning Parnell, the hierarchy declared that on moral grounds he was unfit to remain leader. Gladstone had heeded the sentiments of the most important section of his followers and demanded a temporary retirement at least. His precipitate action in publishing a letter to Parnell after it had failed to convince the Nationalist leader not to seek re-election as chairman hastened on the crisis. Faced with the statement that such an event would render the G.O.M.'s position 'little better than a nullity',[2] the Nationalist majority quailed. Parnell was hoist with his own petard. Liberal party fortunes were waxing, Gladstone appeared to have Home Rule 'in the hollow of his hand', and although Irish nationalism had, as Parnell rightly insisted, not been sapped by material alleviations, the very realism he himself had inculcated into the masses and the party weighed heavily against him. Past neglect of petty

[2] Lyons, *The Fall of Parnell*, p. 85.

matters like the selection of candidates aggravated his difficulties. Lieutenants' nominees tended to follow them into rebellion. O'Shea got his decree on 17th November, 1890. On 6th December, 45 Nationalist M.P.'s repudiated their leader. It is untrue to say, with Emmet Larkin, that for the first time in history the two dominant forces of Catholicism and Nationalism came to a parting of the ways.[3] Apart from the fact of earlier disagreements the issue was not between Catholicism and Nationalism, but between two sets of Nationalists, one of which was backed by the Catholic hierarchy and the overwhelming proportion of the priesthood. Nor is it correct to assert, as does C. C. O'Brien, that the priests' motives were primarily non-political.[4] The evidence clearly proves politics loomed very large in their thoughts. What is true is that the hierarchy very shrewdly said it was playing politics for non-political reasons. The hard fact was Parnell's work was torn to shreds. Basically the crisis was the Galway crisis writ large and in *reverse*. 'So foul a sky clears not without a storm.'

Parnell made the very best of a bad job. His personal involvement was obviously more intense than it had been

[3] Larkin, 'The Roman Catholic Hierarchy, and the Fall of Parnell', *Victorian Studies*, 1961, p. 316.

[4] C. C. O'Brien, op. cit., p. 333–4. See, for instance, the view of Archbishop Croke. C. C. O'Brien, op. cit., p. 291. A quite remarkable pronouncement by another archbishop strikes the reader as not primarily concerned with morals. Archbishop Logue, writing to Archbishop Walsh from Milan, declared: 'A man having the destinies of a people in his hands and bartering it away for the company of an old woman is certainly not a person to beget confidence.' Larkin, 'The Roman Catholic Hierarchy and the Fall of Parnell', *Victorian Studies*, 1961, p. 334.

before, but he played every possible card with immense resource and aplomb. To the cry of the Liberal alliance in danger and the warning as to how terrible for the evicted tenants a Liberal defeat at the next general election would be, he countered the emotive slogan of 'No English Dictation'. He became what he had always condemned—an 'Impossiblist', harking back to the pre-party period and neo-Fenianism. To tighten his hold on the urban artisans he suddenly embraced much of the social and economic reform long advocated by Davitt in the 'Labour World' and even accepted the theory of land nationalization to facilitate raising support in the countryside. Greater emphasis was given by the Parnellites to industrial rejuvenation and a new streamlined agriculture than had been usual from official party spokesmen in the past.[5] One big factor working in Parnell's favour was the attitude of Dillon and W. O'Brien, both of whom had been in the United States on a new fund raising tour when the storm had broken. Defeat for his candidate at the Kilkenny by-election, late in December 1890, induced Parnell to discuss reunion and an agreed withdrawal. As in the party meetings immediately prior to the split he cheated right and left. Nevertheless, while the so-called Boulogne negotiations came to nothing and Dillon and O'Brien reaffirmed their adherence to the Anti-Parnellite cause, Parnell scored one big victory over Gladstone. Early in December 1890 the Liberal leader had contumaciously refused to offer guarantees as to the contents of the next Home Rule Bill while the Irish leadership was in question. Severe attacks on Gladstone in Parnell's

[5] Lyons, 'The Economic Ideas of Parnell', *Historical Studies,* II, ed. Roberts, pp. 73–75.

first great broadside on 29th November 1890 had caused great offence to the whole Liberal leadership.[6] By the end of January 1891 these guarantees had been given. So great had the need to defeat Parnell become and so great had his will to fight and capacity for resistance been shown to be, that a major climb down proved unavoidable. It was made in a bid to secure his peaceful withdrawal, but characteristically, once victorious he adopted a fresh defiant tack. From then on it was a fight to the death. Clashes in parliament were as nothing in comparison with those in Ireland. Scenes of violence and bitterness characterized two more by-elections at North Sligo in April, and Carlow in July, 1891. Apart from the politics, morality and personal conduct were endlessly under discussion. The Captain's 'Lady' and Judy O'Grady were declared 'sisters under the skin'. Sick in body and spirit Parnell found the whole tragedy too much to bear. His marriage to Mrs. O'Shea did not save him. On 6th October, 1891 he died. His enemies had prevailed at last—through his great error. So adept at exploiting weaknesses in others, he had been downed by the same technique. In a manner of speaking he died, politically at least, by his own hand.

Not long before his death Parnell told R. Barry O'Brien he had never 'gone for separation'.[7] If this was so, impracticality was the reason why. He knew his party could never muster the strength to make the British bow so low. Within the limits of the possible, however, he was highly emotional and basically uncontrolled. His arrogance misled. Gladstone was deceived into thinking the signs of excitement shown by the Irish leader

[6] Lyons, *The Fall of Parnell,* pp. 98–117.
[7] R. Barry O'Brien, op. cit., p. 336.

in parliament were false. Yet, as Castlereagh had proved, to be emotional a man does not have to warm in his manner. Passionate arrogance was bound to lead him into the maximum defiance if the way to his ends was blocked. Concessions he took as his right. Toleration was for him a necessary compromise with error. He was a Nehru or Makarios working within the British constitution, rather than a precursor of Botha, Smuts or Cosgrave. Gladstone and Rhodes thought him eminently reasonable. Was not this the initial impression made by Hitler upon Neville Chamberlain? He might have defended any successful Home Rule settlement against the hillside men, just as De Valera quarrelled with the I.R.A. That would not necessarily have meant he had belatedly become a loyal subject of Queen Victoria. More probably he would have been watching and waiting for her to fall upon bad times. That was what the Unionists thought and those who are hated must not make mistakes. Parnell forgot that.

Epilogue

Exit Parnell and Nationalist Ireland lost its only first-class leader of the time. The irony was that his memory remained for almost a decade the major obstacle in the way of unity between the constitutionalist groups and the recreation of the Nationalist party into an instrument with a proper chance of exploiting political opportunities. Gladstone became in effect the man to whom the Anti-Parnellites looked for guidance, especially as he made a second though unsuccessful, attempt to push through Home Rule in 1893; while the loyal remnant of Parnellites either lived on the past, acting as they thought their dead leader would have wished them to do, or gravitated away from strictly constitutional concepts into contempt for the majority they could not master. The trap which caught Parnell had caught them too. Reunion of the sections in 1900 did not succeed in banishing the past and exorcizing faction. Redmond was no 'Uncrowned King', great though his integrity, ability and prestige undoubtedly were. The Liberal alliance had lost much of its immediate value when Rosebery took Gladstone's place in 1894. No obvious gain resulted from the troubled period for Liberalism ending with the succession of Campbell-

Bannerman to the leadership, nor from the Liberal landslide of 1906 from which sprang the Home Rule scheme of 1907—a proposal truly Chamberlainite in its essential features.

Apart from the comparatively short and lamentably weak Gladstone and Rosebery ministries of 1892–95, Unionism ruled the parliamentary roost from the Home Rule split until 1906. The policy of attempting to kill Nationalism by kindness made some progress, albeit on a temporary basis, in that men who began to have something to lose once Land Purchase became widespread were doubly cautious before embarking upon 'trouble'. Then too Balfour's firmness through the 1887 Act in the coercion of violence had taught the generations then mature the reality of British power. Nevertheless, the Fenian tradition lived on and Parnell's tragedy did much to vilify the Liberal alliance in the eyes of Irish Catholic youth. The very aim of 'Killing Home Rule by Kindness' and the milder spirit of Unionist administration in the 1895–1905 period encouraged the belief among the young that a good strong heave would push the British back across the Irish Sea and put paid to Orangeism for ever. Healy's joke about the Anti-Parnellites having the fathers and the Parnellites the sons had a very serious side to it. And when peasant ownership was accompanied by an improvement in agricultural profits and prospects, the wilder men remained unimpressed—saying that independence would bring even more. Quite unabashed by their minority status, suspicious of the Catholic priesthood and hopeful of the efficacy of force, many of the Parnellite persuasion were ripe for conversion to an out-and-out separation movement with a fully independent and tariff-protected Irish Republic as its major goal.

Parnell had joined the United Irishmen, Young Ireland and the Irish Republican Brotherhood as a symbol of separate national identity achieved through bloody struggle. All the realism which had tempered his own deepest yearnings was set at naught in the minds of the extremist groups. Henceforth the dethroned and deceased 'Uncrowned King' was two things at once, for the moderates continued to regard him as their patron saint and in their turn also came to distort his part in the Irish national struggle. Instead of being himself— an extreme man with an acute sense of the possible—he was made either into a Wolfe Tone or a bigger and better Redmond. For the Wolfe Toners the foundation in 1898 of a newspaper called the 'United Irishman' by one Arthur Griffith and the propagation in it of a policy later known as Sinn Fein ('Ourselves') seemed to open up fresh and exciting possibilities. 'Ninety-Eight Clubs', started to commemorate the 1798 rebellion a century after its outbreak, the success they met with and the election in his absence of Arthur Lynch, serving against the British in South Africa, as M.P. for Galway all indicated Griffith had plenty of potential bricks with which to build a new national citadel. But Griffith had persuaded himself that when the Irish members at Westminster had become converts to his creed and withdrew, according to his plan, back to Ireland, met there and directed the administration of the island, the imperial power would voluntarily give up, taking bag and baggage back to Britain. Daring non-violence had not hitherto been the principal hallmark of Irish nationalism and from James Connolly of the new Irish Socialist Republican party came the fresh element of direct force which was to loom so large in the developed Sinn Fein movement. Protection, a hobby-horse of Parnell's, was prominent in the Griffith programme, for under it Ireland was to become a highly developed industrial state. But though much of the Griffith and Connolly creeds was not within immediate reach, or even possible of attainment, the moods they represented were real enough and stirred the plentiful Fenian and Parnellite embers into fresh flame. By the second decade of the twentieth century the different elements in this latest new departure had fused together to create a wealth of revolutionary excitement.

In the very first year of that decade the British electorate played effectively into Irish Nationalist party hands by returning a House of Commons so constituted as to give the Redmond party the same position of holding the balance Parnell had planned so hard to get and actually got earlier on. Immediately the Home Rule cause gathered strength and Redmond's continued aid was made conditional upon the active pursuit of a Home Rule policy by the Asquith government of Liberals and its Labour supporters. Campbell-Bannerman's successor as Liberal leader was if anything less keen on Irish Nationalism than any post-Gladstone chief, but to him it fell to deliver goods others had managed to withhold—a fully-fledged Home Rule Bill. But the gain was ultimately not Redmond's. Again there is a twist of irony in the story, for the fact that the former Parnellite leader should be the man to be outbidden by groups looking among others to Parnell as an inspiration for extreme action is not without its own grim humour. Liberal vacillation, Unionist resistance to the point of armed drilling and Redmond's inability to steer entirely clear of compromise all weakened the moderate

Irish Nationalist groups in Parliament and out. Although
Home Rule went nominally onto the statute book in 1914,
it was in practice still unattained. And while the outbreak of
war in that year and Redmond's grand gesture of loyalty were
initially responded to well, official actions in relation to Ireland
and Irish troops rapidly restored the initiative to Sinn Fein.
Bungle *par excellence*—the mishandling of the small extremist
rising of Easter 1916—effectively cut the ground from beneath
the old Nationalist party's feet. The future was to lay with
armed 'Hillside Men', not argumentative 'Gombeen Men'!
Of course, the rebels could ultimately have been crushed by
British and Ulster force, but in a manner of speaking Griffith
proved to have been right. The British did indeed withdraw
and agreed to a treaty, and did so partly because of the moral
appeal of the Irish cause and abhorrence among British public
opinion at bloodshed and repression. Yet it had needed an
initial Irish use of force to set the process moving, and in this
the old Wolfe Tone method had proved its worth. Then too,
the treaty was made on very stiff conditions and meant Ireland
was partitioned, leaving its principal industrial portions within the reduced United Kingdom. British might and Ulster
right had stood in the way of the march of a nation. Parnell
had been finally thwarted. The tragedy ending at Glasnevin
remained and still remains incompletely avenged. The messiah
has yet to come who can lure the Protestant birds from off
their Unionist trees and into the Dublin nest. Maybe, if he
does appear, his task will only be successfully accomplished
through first agreeing to re-enter some sort of London nest
himself. Meanwhile in Belfast many continue to wear the
sashes their fathers wore.

Appendix

In his life of Cardinal Manning (at pp. 187–90), V. A. McLelland raises some cogent objections to Howard's contention in his article 'The Parnell Manifesto of 21 November, 1885, and the Schools Question' (*E.H.R.*, 1947) that 'Manning's action in the help he gave to the return of Salisbury is to be interpreted wholly in the light of the educational problems of the Catholic Church', though McClelland confuses the 'National Councils' scheme with Home Rule proper. Apart from the Errington Mission dispute and the attempt to get Moran of Sydney appointed Archbishop of Dublin, the failure of the 'National Councils' scheme and the great and growing power of the Nonconformists and secularist Radicals within the Liberal party were such as to push Manning against Gladstone. Moreover, the contention that the Catholic hierarchy subordinated Irish to English questions during the 1885 general election is strongly contradicted by what Manning told Archbishop Walsh. 'I will say at once that I know of no one who desires to subordinate the Irish movement to any English

question' and '*You may rely on me* for refusing to subordinate
the Irish movement to any English question.' McClelland is
certainly correct in saying Howard's statement that the
Catholic clergy 'were primarily concerned not with the
demand for Home Rule, but the threat . . . to the Church's
schools' is not 'very convincing'. In fact it is rather rash, bear-
ing in mind the nature of the relationship between the clergy
and their flocks and the zealous Nationalism of the Irish voters
in Britain.

Even more rash is the further contention that the Irish
Nationalist voters themselves shared this alleged preference of
concern with their priests. 'A study,' he writes, 'of what
actually occurred in the constituencies after the publication of
the manifesto does not confirm the story of Parnell's omnipo-
tence. It shows, on the contrary, that Parnell was obeyed only
in so far as his orders to vote against liberals and radicals
coincided with the advice that Irish Catholics were receiving
from their clergy' (*E.H.R.*, 1947, p. 44). These same voters
had been the ones to push Parnell ahead at the expense of Butt
in 1877 and support any moves for the Home Rule cause taken
by Parnell after he became leader of the Irish Nationalist party.
At the Home Rule election of 1886 and during the years that
followed the Irish voters faithfully supported the Gladstonian Liberals, although the educational problem remained a
bone of contention. Chamberlain's secession in 1886 certainly
eased Liberal-Nationalist relations, but not, as suggested by
Howard, because the Chamberlainite line on education carried
less weight inside the Liberal party thereafter. On the contrary, the Whig secession left the 'Unauthorised Programmers'
in a much stronger position. Does not Howard know that the

N.L.F. preferred to follow Gladstone rather than Chamberlain and that the latter found himself largely forsaken by his one-time cronies in 1886?

In 1885, of course, most of the Irish were being given identical instructions by Parnell and priests alike. Howard therefore seeks to prove his point by dealing with the handful of cases where Parnell instructed his people to vote for Liberals and the larger number of instances where they voted Liberal regardless. Over the first category, consisting of four constituencies, the evidence produced is a little thin. In Northampton there was scarcely any Irish vote. In Newcastle complaints of clerical opposition were to be expected and no proof of their effectiveness is produced. At Sunderland 'a crowded meeting of Irish voters agreed to carry out instructions, but a letter to the local newspaper reported a number of defections'. Well, one would expect the priests to influence a limited number anyway. In Durham the Liberals were defeated and their local newspaper blamed Irish abstentions—stressing Nationalist organizational deficiencies. Here again, the result is not all that of a surprise. After all, with Parnell's spokesmen weak, the clergy had a much greater chance of success. As regards rebellions to the left, it is surely very difficult to prove they were due to priestly instructions? Even on Howard's evidence the nature of the Liberal candidate counted a great deal. If the Liberal candidate was known to favour Catholic causes and Irish aspirations many of the more simple-minded and hot-headed Irish voters would naturally have found voting Conservative a deal too subtle for their tastes. Moreover, a high proportion of this type of rebellion was in London where the priests were far less powerful than in the provinces.

Maybe one or two Liberals supporting Home Rule—and only five Liberal candidates in all openly advocated its adoption—were unable to cajole the Irish voters into coming out in their support. Maybe Davitt was impotent in urging support of socialistic candidates, but Howard has not produced an example of a Liberal clearly opposing Home Rule who received the Irish vote. That would be a real proof of the old priest being writ larger in the Irish voters' mind than new Parnell. Generally speaking Parnell's authority would appear to have been flouted when flouted at all more on lay than ecclesiastical grounds. Fenianism had flourished in the face of priestly displeasure and so did Home Rule. Then too, what about the priests who were prepared to support Liberals? They knew that although some particular men might be 'sound' on Catholic educational aspirations their party would vote them down when the issues came to the fore. Surely these priests were to some extent influenced by the affiliations and sympathies of the candidates concerned with and for Ireland? Nationalism is seldom logical and very seldom used with a nice sense of strategic or tactical advantage. The Howard case would therefore seem very much open to question.

Select Bibliography

All parts of this book—introduction, main text and epilogue—have been influenced by wide reading on Irish history over the past decade. The main arguments, however, can be said to be based on ideas prompted in one way or another by matter to be found in the works listed below.

ARNSTEIN, W. L., 'Parnell and the Bradlaugh Case', *Irish Historical Studies*, 1963.

— *The Bradlaugh Case: A Study in Late Victorian Opinion and Politics* (Oxford, 1965).

BECKETT, J. C., *The Making of Modern Ireland, 1603–1923* (London, 1966).

BRYCE, J. (ed.), *Two Centuries of Irish History, 1691–1870* (London, 1888).

CURTIS, L. P. (Jr.), 'Government Policy and the Irish Party Crisis', *Irish Historical Studies*, 1963.

ENSOR, SIR R. C. K., *England, 1870–1914* (Oxford, 1936).

— 'Some Political and Economic Interactions in Later Victorian England', *Transactions of the Royal Historical Society*, 1949.

GLASER, J. F., 'Parnell's Fall and the Nonconformist Conscience', *Irish Historical Studies*, 1960.

HOWARD, C. H. D., 'Joseph Chamberlain, W. H. O'Shea, and Parnell, 1884, 1891–2', *Irish Historical Studies*, 1962.

— 'The Parnell Manifesto of 21 November 1885 and the Schools Question', *English Historical Review*, 1947.

HURST, M. C., 'Ireland and the Ballot Act of 1872', *Historical Journal*, 1964.

LARKIN, E., 'Mounting the Counter-Attack: The Roman Catholic Hierarchy and the Destruction of Parnellism', *The Review of Politics*, 1963.

— 'The Roman Catholic Hierarchy and the Fall of Parnell', *Victorian Studies*, 1961.

LECKY, W. E. H., *Leaders of Public Opinion in Ireland* (new edition, London, 1903).

LYONS, F. S. L., *Parnell*, Irish History Series No. 3 (Dundalk, 1965). Published for the Dublin Historical Association.

— 'The Economic Ideas of Parnell', *Historical Studies*, II. Edited by M. Roberts. (Being papers read to the third conference of Irish historians.) (London, 1959.)

— *The Fall of Parnell* (London, 1960).

MACINTYRE, A., *The Liberator: Daniel O'Connell and the Irish Party, 1830–1847* (London, 1965).

MANSERGH, N., *The Irish Question, 1840–1921* (London, 1965).

MCDOWELL, R. B., *Public Opinion and Government Policy in Ireland, 1801–1846* (London, 1952).

MOODY, T. W., 'Parnell and the Galway Election of 1886', *Irish Historical Studies*, 1951.

— 'The New Departure in Irish Politics, 1878–9', *Essays in British and Irish History in Honour of James Eadie Todd*, edited by H. A. Cronne, T. W. Moody and D. B. Quinn (London, 1949).

NOWLAN, K. B., *The Politics of Repeal: A Study in the Relations between Great Britain and Ireland, 1841–50* (London, 1965).

O'BRIEN, C. C., *Parnell and his Party, 1880–90* (Oxford, 1957).

O'BRIEN, C. C. (ed.), *The Shaping of Modern Ireland* (London, 1960).

O'BRIEN, R. B., *The Life of Charles Stewart Parnell*, 2 vols. (London, 1899).

O'CONNOR, SIR J., *History of Ireland, 1798–1924*, 2 vols. (London, 1926).

STRAUSS, E., *Irish Nationalism and British Democracy* (London, 1951).

THORNLEY, D., *Isaac Butt and Home Rule* (London, 1964).

— 'The Irish Home Rule Party and Parliamentary Obstruction, 1874–1887', Historical Revision: XI, *Irish Historical Studies*, 1960.

WHYTE, J. H., *The Independent Irish Party, 1850–9* (Oxford, 1958).

Index

All persons referred to below are given the descriptions applying to them in the years dealt with by this book, or, when not contemporaries, those now usually employed for them.

Index

Index

Index